CW01430820

Mesopotamian History Trivia

Explore the Cradle of Civilization with 500+ Questions and Answers About Ancient Mesopotamia

© Copyright 2024 - All rights reserved.

The content contained within this book may not be reproduced, duplicated, or transmitted without direct written permission from the author or the publisher.

Under no circumstances will any blame or legal responsibility be held against the publisher or author for any damages, reparation, or monetary loss due to the information contained within this book, either directly or indirectly.

Legal Notice:

This book is copyright-protected. It is only for personal use. You cannot amend, distribute, sell, use, quote, or paraphrase any part of the content within this book without the consent of the author or publisher.

Disclaimer Notice:

Please note the information contained within this document is for educational and entertainment purposes only. All effort has been executed to present accurate, up-to-date, reliable, and complete information. No warranties of any kind are declared or implied. Readers acknowledge that the author is not engaging in the rendering of legal, financial, medical, or professional advice. The content within this book has been derived from various sources. Please consult a licensed professional before attempting any techniques outlined in this book.

By reading this document, the reader agrees that under no circumstances is the author responsible for any losses, direct or indirect, that are incurred as a result of the use of the information contained within this document, including, but not limited to, errors, omissions, or inaccuracies.

Welcome Aboard, Check Out This Limited-Time Free Bonus!

Ahoy, reader! Welcome to the Ahoy Publications family, and thanks for snagging a copy of this book! Since you've chosen to join us on this journey, we'd like to offer you something special.

Check out the link below for a FREE e-book filled with delightful facts about American History.

But that's not all - you'll also have access to our exclusive email list with even more free e-books and insider knowledge. Well, what are ye waiting for? Click the link below to join and set sail toward exciting adventures in American History.

Access your bonus here

https://ahoypublications.com/

Or, Scan the QR code!

Table of Contents

Introduction

Ancient Mesopotamia, the land known for its productive territories and some of humanity's greatest inventions, has many treasures to uncover. For thousands of years B.C.E., Mesopotamians lived through challenging times and had many victories, on and off the battleground.

From this trivia collection book, you'll learn how the Mesopotamians grew their power and culture, from a few small settlements between two rivers to the greatest empires in the ancient world. You'll discover how these empires fell and everything that happened on the battlefields and in the lives of everyday people.

You'll read about the ancient gods and goddesses, rulers, builders, and inventors who allowed the Mesopotamian civilizations to become the magnificent empires they were known throughout history. You'll also see how the ancient Mesopotamian civilization influenced the modern world – and not just in its present-day territory.

Are you new to history trivia or ancient civilization trivia? Don't worry. This book is excellent for beginners because it has simple explanations for all questions – even the most challenging ones.

Not only that, but some of the questions are easy to answer once you take a little time to think about them. If you haven't read a history trivia book before, start with these.

You can have several tries at solving a question, so don't worry if you don't get it right the first time. You can go back as many times as you remember something interesting you read.

At the end of each chapter, you'll find the answer keys. If you don't know the answer to a question, resist the temptation of jumping right to the answer. Stop and think a little more before looking up the answer.

If you read trivia books regularly, you'll enjoy some of the more challenging questions, too. After all, trivia is only fun if it makes you work hard on figuring out the answers. When you do, you'll feel like you're on top of the world.

If you want to share all the fun facts you've learned, feel free to read them to others. One of the best things about this book is that you can share it with anyone. No matter how much they know about ancient Mesopotamia, they'll have just as much fun reading the questions and answers.

Some of the answers will surprise you – and will surprise others if you read them too. You can have fun with friends and family and more gems from your historical treasure chest. It's the best of both worlds.

Want to know why this book is great for everyone? It doesn't only have boring historical facts you're used to seeing in their history book. It has sidebars and fact boxes with fun facts you may never have heard of before, so you won't be bored.

Are you ready to start your journey through the mysterious ancient Mesopotamia? If so, go ahead and continue reading. Each chapter will reveal a hidden gem (or maybe several gems) you can share or put away to build your knowledge of ancient history.

Chapter 1: The Dawn of Mesopotamian Civilization

According to the earliest historical records, life in ancient Mesopotamia began thriving around 8000 B.C.E. However, it's possible that people lived in this territory long before this date. After all, it was located between two large rivers, which made the land perfect for growing crops and raising animals for food, clothes, and more.

To start our journey, this chapter will show you how the Mesopotamian civilizations grew in the beginning and how this affected the lives of Mesopotamian people.

Multiple Choice Questions

1. What are the two major rivers that defined the borders of Mesopotamia?

   A. Nile and Amazon

   B. Tigris and Euphrates

   C. Ganges and Yangtze

   D. White Nile and Blue Nile

2. Which modern languages is the Akkadian language related to?

   A. Arabic

   B. Hebrew

   C. Burmese

   D. Khmer

3. What was the Code of Hammurabi written on?

    A. Papyrus

    B. Clay tablets and stone slabs

    C. Papyrus and clay tablets

    D. Stone tablets

4. The Code of Hammurabi determined punishment for crimes based on what?

    A. The crime

    B. The time the crime was committed

    C. Social status

    D. The age of the accused

5. The Code of Hammurabi was an early form of constitutional government because it contained what?

    A. The chance for people to present evidence in their case

    B. The presumption of innocence until proven guilty

    C. Adjustments based on social status

    D. All of the above

6. Which were the main social classes in ancient Mesopotamia?

    A. Kings, priests, lower classes, and slaves

    B. Kings, scribes, and slaves

    C. Rulers, the middle class, and slaves

    D. Rulers, priests, and scribes

7. Which language replaced the Sumerian language after 2004 B.C.E.?

    A. Akkadian

    B. Assyrian

    C. Amorite

    D. Semirite

8. Who was Sargon of Akkad?

    A. Akkadian ruler

    B. The ruler who transformed Sumer, the small city-state, into the world's first empire

    C. Assyrian ruler

    D. A ruler chosen by gods

9. Who were the most powerful enemies of the Akkadians?

    A. Persians

    B. Macedonians

    C. Egyptians

    D. The citizens of the city-state of Ebla

10. Which rival civilization did the Sumerians influence the most?

    A. The city-state of Ebla

    B. The Elamites

    C. The Egyptians

    D. The Indus Valley Civilization

True or False

1. The Mesopotamians were the first to create a written code of laws.

- True
- False

2. The Mesopotamians were one of the first urban, specialized societies.

- True
- False

3. The early Mesopotamian civilization was a mixture of the two neighboring civilizations.

- True
- False

4. Cuneiform writing was only used briefly in the 21st century B.C.E.

- True
- False

5. The Sumerians started trading with other early civilizations on land.

- True
- False

6. The world's first dynastic empire was the Sumerian.

- True
- False

7. The Assyrian Empire was named after its capital city.

- True
- False

8. The Assyrian empire was smaller than the Akkadian empire.

- True
- False

9. Babylon was a small city for over a century before it became the center of the famous Babylonian empire.

- True
- False

10. The Babylonian empire was finally destroyed by the Persians.

- True
- False

Fill-in-the-Blank

1. The term Mesopotamian means the land _____ _____ _____.

2. The world's oldest known city, _____, was located in ancient Mesopotamia.

3. One of the most important Mesopotamian inventions was _____.

4. Besides legal codes and writing, the Mesopotamians were also known for their use of _____.

5. _____ played an important role in Mesopotamian culture and life.

6. One of the world's first most famous stories, The Epic of Gilgamesh, was written in _____.

7. Mesopotamians used cuneiform writing to write down _____ and _____ to one another and record _____ and _____.

8. The Sumerians were excellent _____-builders, creating vessels to travel across the _____.

9. Sumerian religion was _____, and their gods often had _____ form.

10. In Sumer, the centers of the cities were the temples, built on enormous _____.

Picture-Based Questions

1. What is the name of this ancient form of writing developed in Mesopotamia?

Illustration 1

Response: _____

2. Sumerian writing wasn't only used for records. This plaque is from around 2600 B.C.E. and has writing and pictures on it. Can you guess what it was used for?

Illustration 2

Response:

_____

_____

_____

3. Name this ancient Mesopotamian structure.

Illustration 3

Response: _____

4. Which Mesopotamian Empire is shown in green?

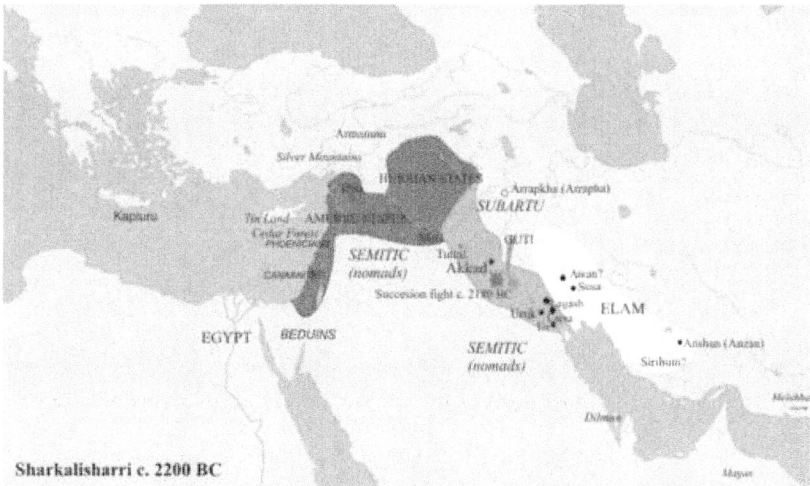

Illustration 4

Response: _____

5. This conqueror caused the end of the remaining Mesopotamian culture. Who was he?

Illustration 5

Response: _____

6. This Mesopotamian Empire was founded after an uprising, which brought the second code of law from ancient Mesopotamia. Can you name it?

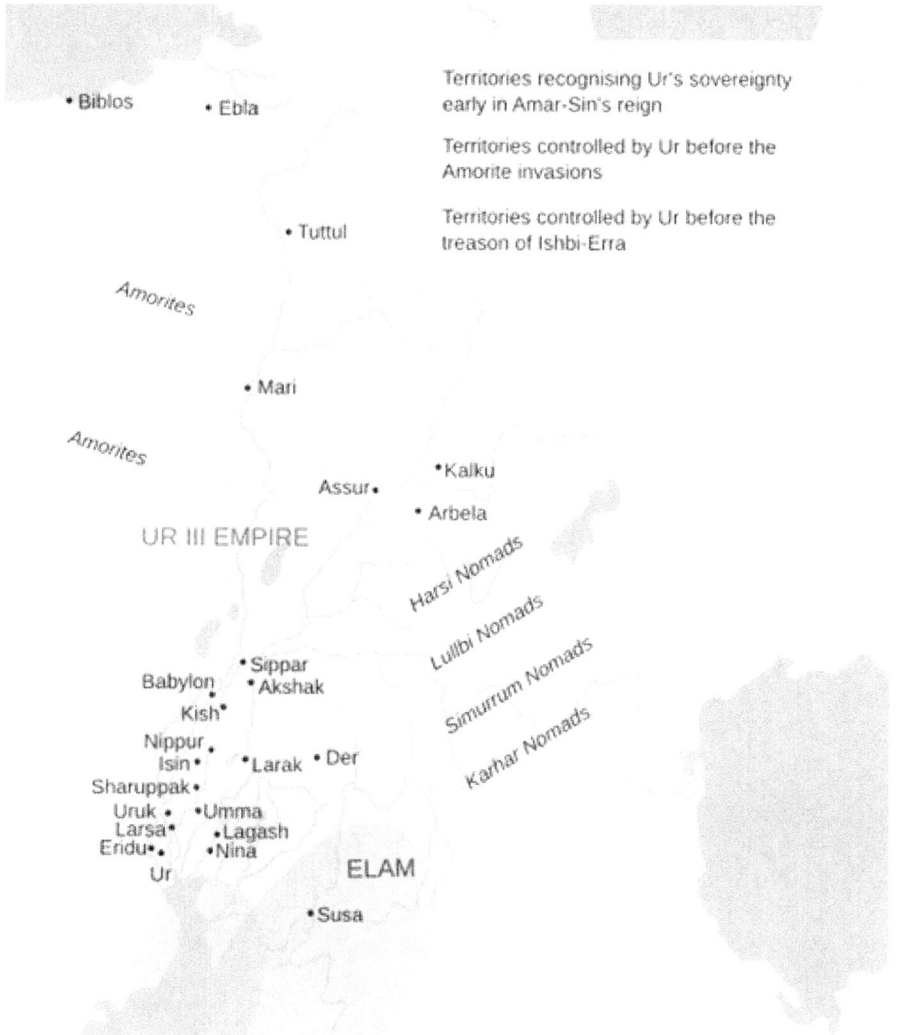

• Biblos   • Ebla

Territories recognising Ur's sovereignty early in Amar-Sin's reign

Territories controlled by Ur before the Amorite invasions

• Tuttul

Territories controlled by Ur before the treason of Ishbi-Erra

Amorites

• Mari

Amorites

•Kalku

Assur•

• Arbela

UR III EMPIRE

Harsi Nomads

Lulibi Nomads

•Sippar

Babylon   • Akshak

Simurrum Nomads

Kish•

Nippur•

Karhar Nomads

Isin•   •Larak   • Der

Sharuppak•

Uruk • •Umma

Larsa•   •Lagash

Eridu•. •Nina

Ur

ELAM

•Susa

Illustration 6

Response: _____

7. What does this map from the 17th century B.C.E. represent?

Illustration 7

Response:

_____

_____

_____

8. These pictures show Mesopotamian helmets as depicted in ancient clay reliefs (tablets). Can you guess which empire these helmets were used in?

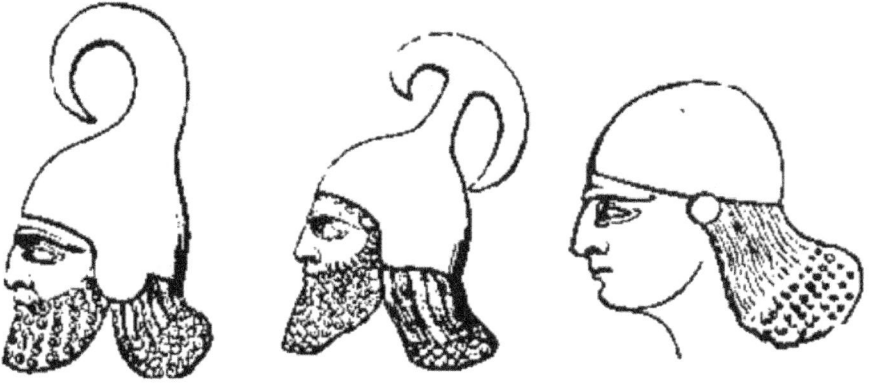

Illustration 8

Response: _____

9. Name this Mesopotamian ruler who came to power in the new dynasty in 722 B.C.E.

Illustration 9

Response: _____

10. Name the Mesopotamian city where this ancient gate is located.

Illustration 10

Response: _____

Timeline Questions

1. Arrange these Mesopotamian empires in chronological order:

- Babylonian
- Sumerian
- Akkadian
- Assyrian

2. Arrange these events in chronological order:

- First larger civilization appears
- Earliest civilizations form in Mesopotamia
- First recorded writing
- Agriculture becomes common

3. Arrange these Sumerian events in chronological order:

- The oldest wheel
- Cultural interchange with the Akkadians begins
- The approximate date of the writing of the Epic of Gilgamesh
- Sumerians are under the rule of the Akkadian Empire

4. Arrange the following events in chronological order:

- Babylonians conquer southern Mesopotamian
- The collapse of the Akkadian Empire
- Babylon is founded
- The rule of the Assyrian Empire

5. Arrange the following Babylonian events in order:

- The Rise of the Neo-Babylonian Empire
- Code of Hammurabi is written
- The first invasion of Babylon
- Persians conquer Babylon

6. Which came first, the rise of agriculture or the growth of the cities?

7. Did the Sumerians write on clay tablets first and later baked the tablets or carved their symbols onto already baked tablets?

8. Arrange the events in chronological order:

- Gutian uprising
- The fall of the Akkadian Empire
- The founding of Babylon
- The Sumerians getting under the control of Ur

9. Arrange the events in chronological order:

- The Assyrians conquered the Hittites
- The Hittites conquer Babylon
- The Assyrians conquered Israel
- The dynasty is divided into provinces

10. Which came first, the destruction of the ancient Mesopotamian cities and culture or the defeat of the Persian Empire?

Response: _____

Chapter 2: Gods and Myths: The Mesopotamian Pantheon

The ancient Mesopotamians were polytheistic, meaning they worshiped many gods and goddesses. Some of these deities were local and only known to some groups, while others transcended territory and empires that rose and fell across Mesopotamia.

This chapter will introduce you to Mesopotamian mythology and the roles of the most important gods and goddesses. You can test your knowledge, see how many you have heard of, and learn about the lesser-known ones.

Gods and Goddesses: The Mesopotamian Pantheon

Among the many gods worshiped by the Mesopotamians, three had the most important roles. This trio was made of Anu, the sky god, Ea, the god of water and wisdom, and Enlil, the ruler of fates. Ea was also known as the creator and protector of people, while Enlil ruled the storms and earth.

Ereshkigal and Ishtar were sisters, both important goddesses, often accompanied by shadows and other night animals. They were particularly worshiped in Babylon – each Mesopotamian city had its own patron god or goddess.

Marduk, the firstborn son of Ea, was a hero and a god, who, like his father, showed great strengths. As a reward, he was given the responsibility to control the matters that the higher god ruled over previously.

There were thousands of other deities in the Mesopotamian pantheon, including the lesser gods, who reported to the higher powers. Some were shapeshifters, some were born human and later earned immortality, while others had dark powers and were often depicted as demons.

The stories of Ea's great deeds were seen in the myth of the Great Flood and the Epic of Gilgamesh. In another story, Ea created people by shaping them out of clay and breathing life into them. Enlil, not liking the idea of other beings sharing Eas's essence, sent a flood to destroy humans. Ea told people that if they wanted to survive, they should build an ark —which they did and were saved as a result.

Multiple Choice Questions

1. **Which Mesopotamian god was known as the king of the gods and the god of the sky?**

    A. Enki

    B. Anu

    C. Tiamat

    D. Ea

2. **Anu, Enlil, and Ea presided over which matters?**

    A. Spirits

    B. Lower gods

    C. Universe

    D. All of the above

3. **Sumerian is a...**

    A. Language

    B. Religion

    C. Cult

    D. None of the above

4. What was the domain of Ninib, Shamash, and Nergal?

    A. Water

    B. Sun

    C. Moon

    D. Storm

5. What kind of deities are Ea and Nebo?

    A. Sun

    B. Moon

    C. Water

    D. Land

6. How were the different deities worshiped in different regions of Mesopotamia?

    A. The same way

    B. Differently

    C. Some worshiped the same, others differently

    D. Some regions had specific methods of worship for some gods

7. Which Mesopotamian empire are the "Seven Gods Who Decree" associated with?

    A. Akkadian

    B. Babylonian

    C. Sumerian

    D. Assyrian

8. Which text is central to Mesopotamian mythology, explaining the origins and powers of the most important deities?

    A. Enuma Elish

    B. Epic of Gilgamesh

    C. The family of Mesopotamian gods

    D. Inanna's descent

9. It's impossible to trace back the origin of all Mesopotamian gods and goddesses. Why?

  A. Some appear multiple times

  B. Some are only mentioned vaguely

  C. Some have confusing origins

  D. All of the above

10. Despite all the differences in the portrayal of the various gods and goddesses, there were some constant themes. For example, Nanna and Ningal were always the parents of which deity?

  A. Ea

  B. Dumuzi

  C. Inanna

  D. Antum

True or False

1. The Epic of Gilgamesh is one of the earliest known works of literary fiction.

- True
- False

2. Ea is the other main character in the story *Inanna and the God of Wisdom.*

- True
- False

3. Mesopotamians believed that people were equal to the gods.

- True
- False

4. Stories of destruction by gods are rare in Mesopotamian history.

- True
- False

5. The Mesopotamians believed that the gods would punish them even in the afterlife.

- True
- False

6. The Sumerians had a concept of god from the early days.

- True
- False

7. Many of the Mesopotamian deities were created to explain events people saw occur in their day-to-day lives.

- True
- False

8. The Mesopotamian gods and goddesses often appeared to people.

- True
- False

9. The Mesopotamian pantheon grew as the political and social events evolved throughout the region's history.

- True
- False

10. At the beginning of the second millennium B.C., the Babylonians ranked their major deities in a hierarchical numerical order.

- True
- False

Fill-in-the-Blank

1. The Mesopotamian goddess of love and war is named _____.

2. The Babylonian god of death and illness is called _____.

3. The Sumerians also had another goddess of love. Her name is _____.

4. _____ is one of the seven sages often depicted carrying a bucket and a cone of incense for purification.

5. The Mesopotamian god of sweet and fresh water is _____. He was killed by his son _____.

6. The Babylonians offered their gratitude to _____ when a building was completed.

7. The Sumerian "Mistress of Animals," _____, was a local mother goddess.

8. The Babylonian god of grain and fertility, _____, was worshiped near the midsection of the Euphrates.

9. As the mother of the hero-turned-god Marduk, _____ also had a major role in the Babylonian pantheon.

10. The Babylonian god of wisdom is named _____ or _____.

Picture-Based Questions

1. Identify this deity and describe its role in Mesopotamian mythology.

Illustration 11

Response:

_____

_____

_____

2. Besides deities, other religious figures were also depicted in clay or stone statues in Mesopotamia. Can you guess the role of this figure?

Illustration 12

Response:

_____

_____

_____

3. Name this divine creature from Mesopotamian mythology.

Illustration 13

Response:

_____

_____

_____

4. Name this Mesopotamian god.

Illustration 14

Response:

_____

_____

_____

5. Like many gods, this one also had an animal form. Can you guess who the fish/serpent from the left side of the picture is?

Illustration 15

Response:

_____

_____

_____

6. This Mesopotamian creature was defeated by Gilgamesh and Enkidu. Do you know its name?

Illustration 16

Response:

_____

_____

_____

7. This picture depicts the marriage of which gods?

Illustration 17

Response:

_____

_____

_____

8. This god was worshiped by the Akkadians but was later absorbed into the god Marduk. Who is he?

Illustration 18

Response:

_____

_____

_____

9. Name this goddess.

Illustration 19

Response:

_____

_____

_____

10. Name this Babylonian deity.

Illustration 20

Response:

_____

_____

_____

Match the God to Their Domain

1. Anu	Fire and light
2. Ereshkigal	Death
3. Geshtianna	Grain
4. Damu	Underworld
5. Zababa	Magic
6. Nusku	Sky
7. Nergal	Gate-keeping
8. Haya	War
9. Asalluhi	Healing
10. Papsukkal	Fertility

Chapter 3: Rivers of Life: The Tigris and Euphrates

Due to their location, the rivers of Tigris and Euphrates were able to provide the perfect lifeline for the cradle of civilization. While the Agricultural Revolution started much before the first Mesopotamian empire was founded, this unique place between the twin rivers took the revolution's development to a whole other level.

From this chapter, you'll learn about the role of these rivers in shaping the life and history of the Mesopotamian people.

Multiple Choice Questions

1. Which river was known for its more unpredictable flooding, which was crucial for Mesopotamian agriculture?

    A. The Tigris

    B. The Euphrates

    C. Both rivers equally

    D. A third river

2. What resources did the Mesopotamians find in and near the rivers?

    A. Reed

    B. Fish

    C. Water

    D. All of the above

3. Which trading route did the marshes provide a connection to?

    A. Egyptian

    B. Persian

    C. Macedonian

    D. Indus Valley

4. What other resources did people in Upper Mesopotamian have?

    A. Mountains and forests

    B. Land routes for other resources

    C. Metals

    D. Something else

5. Aided by the water resources, the Agricultural Revolution led to what other event in the history of Mesopotamian civilizations?

    A. Urban Revolution

    B. Industrial Revolution

    C. Violent protests and uprisings

    D. Water travel expansion

6. What efforts did living and working in the retreating wetlands in Lower Mesopotamia require?

    A. Coordination and physical labor

    B. More time spent looking for water

    C. Moving settlements

    D. It didn't require any specific effort

7. Rivers usually drain to the sea. With the Tigris and Euphrates, this was often prevented, causing even more issues for Mesopotamian farmers. What were the reasons for this?

    A. Lack of rainfall

    B. Too much water was used for irrigation

    C. Irregular flooding

    D. Too much rainfall

8. What are the names of some of the wetlands near the rivers in Mesopotamia?

    A. Deltas

    B. Estuaries

    C. Salt marshes

    D. All of the above

9. What type of marshes were available in areas near the Tigris and Euphrates rivers?

    A. Permanent

    B. Permanent and Seasonal

    C. Seasonal

    D. Mixed

10. Why were the marshes important for the development of the Mesopotamian civilizations?

    A. They were used for irrigation

    B. They eliminated the need for irrigation

    C. They made growing healthy crops easier

    D. They collected rainfall

True or False

1. The Mesopotamians built extensive canal systems to control river flooding and irrigate their lands.

- True
- False

2. Climate shifts have also played a role in the development of Mesopotamian civilization.

- True
- False

3. Civilization developed in exactly the same way throughout the region.

- True
- False

4. Despite the drier patches, the Mesopotamian area was still wetter than the rest of the Middle East.

- True
- False

5. Having two rivers to use for watering had put the Mesopotamians to an advantage throughout the entire year.

- True
- False

6. The earliest cities of Mesopotamia developed on the edges of the largest marches near the twin rivers.

- True
- False

7. Irrigation was necessary in all regions.

- True
- False

8. In Sumer, villages evolved into cities before 4000 **B.C.E.**

- True
- False

9. In the beginning, Mesopotamia was suitable land for living and farming, even without irrigation.

- True
- False

10. Due to the slower development in the northern areas, they were overtaken by the southern civilizations.

- True
- False

Fill-in-the-Blank

1. The _____ is an ancient Mesopotamian story that includes a great flood similar to the biblical tale of Noah's Ark.

2. The vicinity of the rivers and wetlands made it easier to organize small-scale _____ irrigation and eliminated the need for _____ water from farther away.

3. In the beginning, Mesopotamian farmers mainly cultivated _____ and _____. Later on, they established _____, where they could also grow beans, peas, lentils, cucumbers, leeks, lettuce, garlic, grapes, apples, melons, and figs.

4. As the Agricultural Revolution continued, the Mesopotamians also began to keep cows, sheep, goats, and cows for their _____ and _____.

5. Each year, the floods of the twin rivers brought _____ to the land – leaving the farmers with a mixture of rich, _____ and _____.

6. In the valleys between the Tigris and the Euphrates, the intense _____ made living and farming even harder without irrigation.

7. Early Mesopotamians learned to adapt to their _____, especially to available _____ _____ that served their community.

8. The first civilization went without rain for _____ months of the year.

9. The development of irrigation also led to a quick _____ development.

10. To ensure the water levels were always balanced in all lands, Mesopotamia farmers often _____ from one water tank into another.

Picture-Based Questions

1. Identify the Tigris and Euphrates rivers on this map.

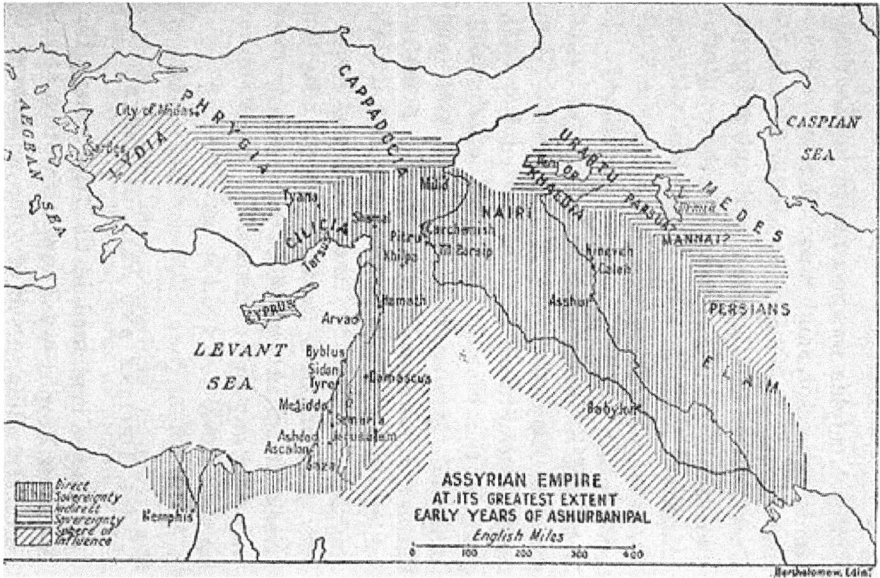

Illustration 21

Response:

_____

_____

_____

2. This area (which includes Mesopotamia and the Tiger and Euphrates rivers) has a unique name. Do you know its name?

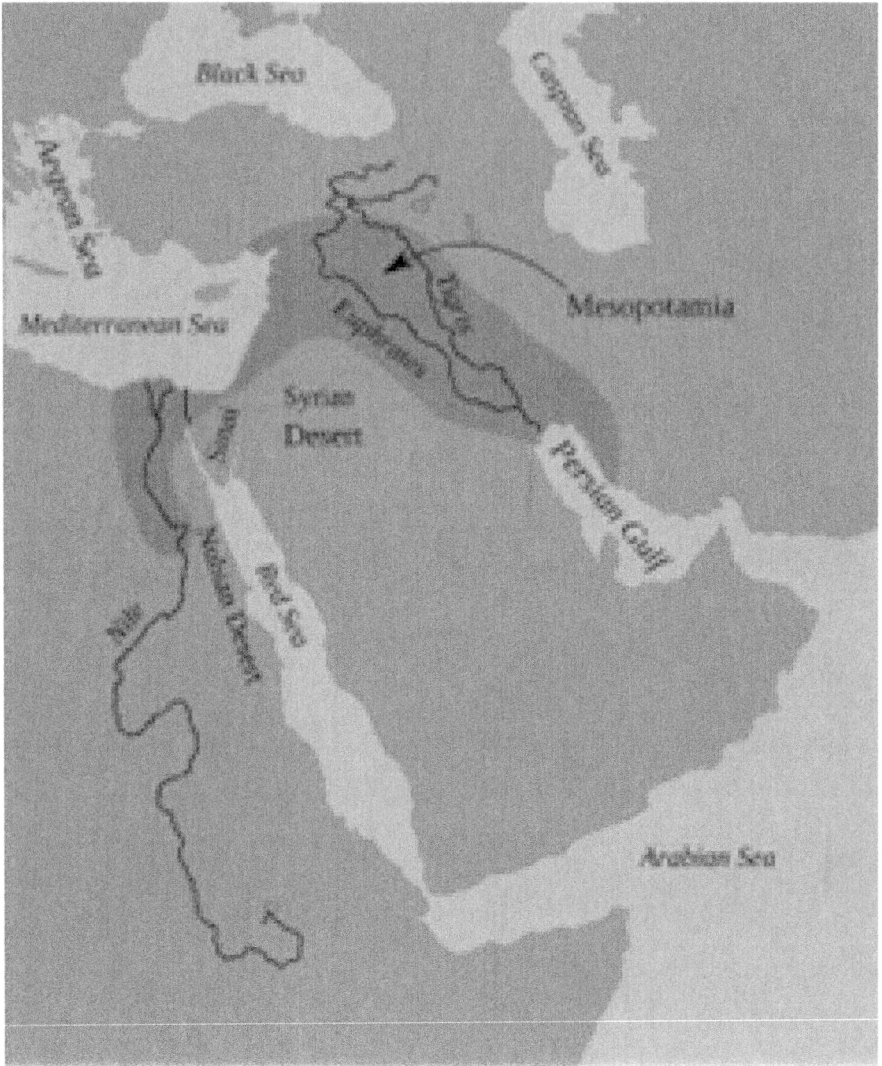

Illustration 22

Response:

_____

_____

_____

3. According to the legends, the burial of the epic hero required the Euphrates to be diverted temporarily. Who was he?

Illustration 23

Response:

_____

_____

_____

4. These areas were common near the Tigris and Euphrates rivers. Do you know what they're called?

Illustration 24

Response:

_____

_____

_____

5. What water-related event is depicted in this picture?

Illustration 25

Response:

_____

_____

_____

6. Besides agriculture, the waters of the two rivers were also used for another important activity. Look at the picture to guess which activity this was.

Illustration 26

Response:

_____

_____

_____

7. This lake is the place of origin for Tigris. What's its name?

Illustration 27

Response: _____

8. What other unique facts can be discovered from this picture of the Tigris and Euphrates? Look at the picture for a hint.

Illustration 28

Response:

_____

_____

_____

9. At the very bank of Euphrates lies the city where the hero Atrahasis was born. Which city was this?

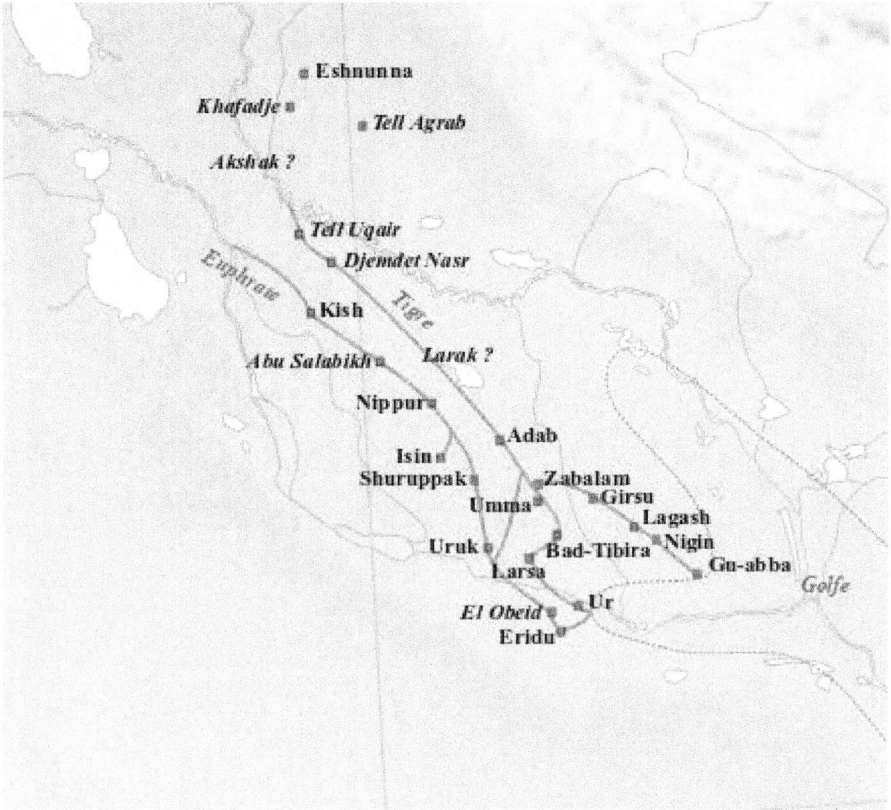

Illustration 29

Response: _____

10. What connection does this picture point to?

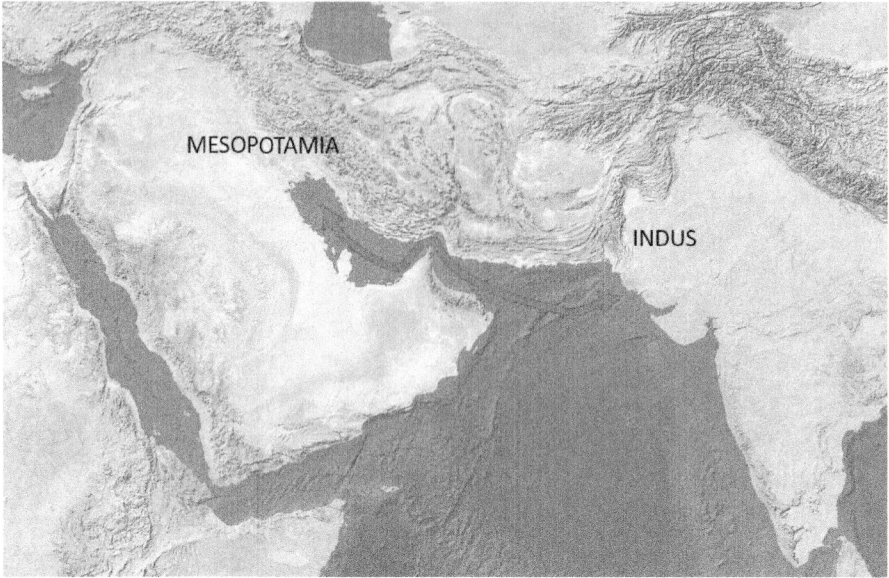

Illustration 30

Response: _____

Short Answer

1. Explain how the Tigris and Euphrates rivers contributed to the success of Mesopotamian agriculture.

_____

_____

_____

2. Which modern-day countries are now in the "land between rivers" (Mesopotamia)?

_____

_____

_____

3. Which famous Mesopotamian city was among the first to have 50,000 inhabitants?

_____

_____

_____

4. How are the Mesopotamian innovations linked to agriculture and the twin rivers?

_____

_____

_____

5. How did life differ in Upper Mesopotamia, where the area was dry and became even drier?

_____

_____

_____

6. What influenced the levels of water in the Tigris and Euphrates rivers?

_____

_____

_____

7. How damaging were the river floodings without intervention?

_____

_____

_____

8. Besides leading water to the fields, what role did the canals have?

_____

_____

_____

9. How else did the Mesopotamians protect themselves and their property from flooding?

_____

_____

_____

10. How did efficient agriculture and water resource use help advance the Mesopotamian civilization?

_____

_____

_____

Chapter 4: Scribes and Scholars: The Invention of Writing

Once upon a time, Mesopotamians found it easier to record information in pictures. However, as their population grew, there were very few people who knew how to interpret these pictures.

According to some historians (not everyone agrees on when and how writing was invented), cuneiform writing was developed as a way to interpret spoken language and to make it easier for everyone to understand written information.

Regardless of its origins, cuneiform was the first official form of writing in human history and a groundbreaking invention that shaped civilizations. This chapter will look at the early days of cuneiform and its practitioners, the scribes, and the scholars.

Dive into this fascinating world to see how writing began and what it looked like in ancient Mesopotamia.

Multiple Choice

1. Cuneiform was primarily written on which material?

A. Papyrus

B. Clay tablets

C. Stone walls

D. Wood pieces

2. The cuneiform wedges were transformed into phonetic records. What does this mean?

    A. The words were written based on sounds

    B. The words were written based on letters

    C. The letters were written based on syllables

    D. The letters were written based on how they would sound individually

3. Who used cuneiform in Mesopotamia?

    A. Merchants and Employers

    B. Priests

    C. Recordkeepers

    D. All of the above

4. What was the earliest form of cuneiform?

    A. Simple lines

    B. Pictures of items

    C. Connected lines

    D. Lines combined with pictures

5. What did the scribes use to make the cuneiform wedges?

    A. A metal tool

    B. Reed stylus cut

    C. Obsidian tool

    D. Feathers

6. Besides Sumerian, in how many languages was cuneiform used throughout its history?

    A. 5

    B. 15

    C. 10

    D. 25

7. The records of which empire are the most complete (to provide the proper chronological order of events of Mesopotamia)?

    A. Sumerian

    B. Babylonia

    C. Akkadian

    D. Assyrian

8. One of the most important cuneiform records from Mesopotamia centers around a planet in the solar system. Which planet is this?

   A. Neptune

   B. Saturn

   C. Venus

   D. Jupiter

9. What made scribes different from everyone else

   A. The ability to read and write

   B. Years of education

   C. Special privileges in society

   D. All of the above

10. What was the building where scribes learned to read and write called?

   A. Tablet House

   B. Scribe House

   C. Learning House

   D. Writing House

True or False

1. The Mesopotamian cuneiform script was used only for religious texts.

   - True

   - False

2. Many sacred texts from Mesopotamia were preserved in cuneiform.

   - True

   - False

3. Rulers also used cuneiform.

   - True

   - False

4. Writing in cuneiform required precise movements.

   - True

   - False

5. Cuneiform writing could've originated from an ancient form of accounting technique.

- True
- False

6. The scribes made uniform marks so everyone who learned them could recognize them.

- True
- False

7. The Epic of Gilgamesh was only written in Sumerian cuneiform.

- True
- False

8. Cuneiform couldn't be used to create complex images of lake maps.

- True
- False

9. Literacy was widespread, and everyone could write cuneiform.

- True
- False

10. There were just as many women scribes as there were men scribes.

- True
- False

Fill-in-the-Blank

1. The famous Mesopotamian ruler, King _____, created one of the earliest law codes written in cuneiform.

2. The term "cuneiform" originates from the Latin cuneus word, which means _____.

3. Writing gives _____ to a symbol, similar to how Mesopotamian priests interpreted _____ _____ for looking into the future.

4. Cuneiform was a very _____ writing system, and some texts could only be written and interpreted by _____.

5. Although created over 4000 years ago, cuneiform writing was only deciphered in _____.

6. Cuneiform writing first appeared in Sumerian cities with _____ economy.

7. Temple officials used cuneiform to record the amount of _____ and the number of _____ leaving or entering their storages.

8. Besides simple recordings like lists, there were also _____ enclosed in _____ envelope.

9. Assyrian kings had _____ full of records in _____ script.

10. The longest cuneiform literary work is the _____ _____ _____.

Picture-Based Questions

1. What type of information might this cuneiform tablet contain?

Illustration 31

Response:

_____

_____

_____

2. This tablet contains a map of a Babylonian city. Which city is it?

Illustration 32

Response:

_____

_____

_____

3. This tablet is different. Can you guess why?

Illustration 33

Response:

_____

_____

_____

4. Early (pictograph) writing looked something like this. This tablet comes from a city where pictographs shifted to true cuneiform writing. Can you guess which city is that?

Illustration 34

Response:

_____

_____

_____

5. This tablet is dedicated to the goddess who became the patron of writing and the scribes. Who was she?

Illustration 35

Response:

_____

_____

_____

6. What was the function of this figure?

Illustration 36

Response: _____

7. When they finished school, young scribes were given a tablet with advice from their former teacher or texts like this. Can you guess what's listed on this tablet?

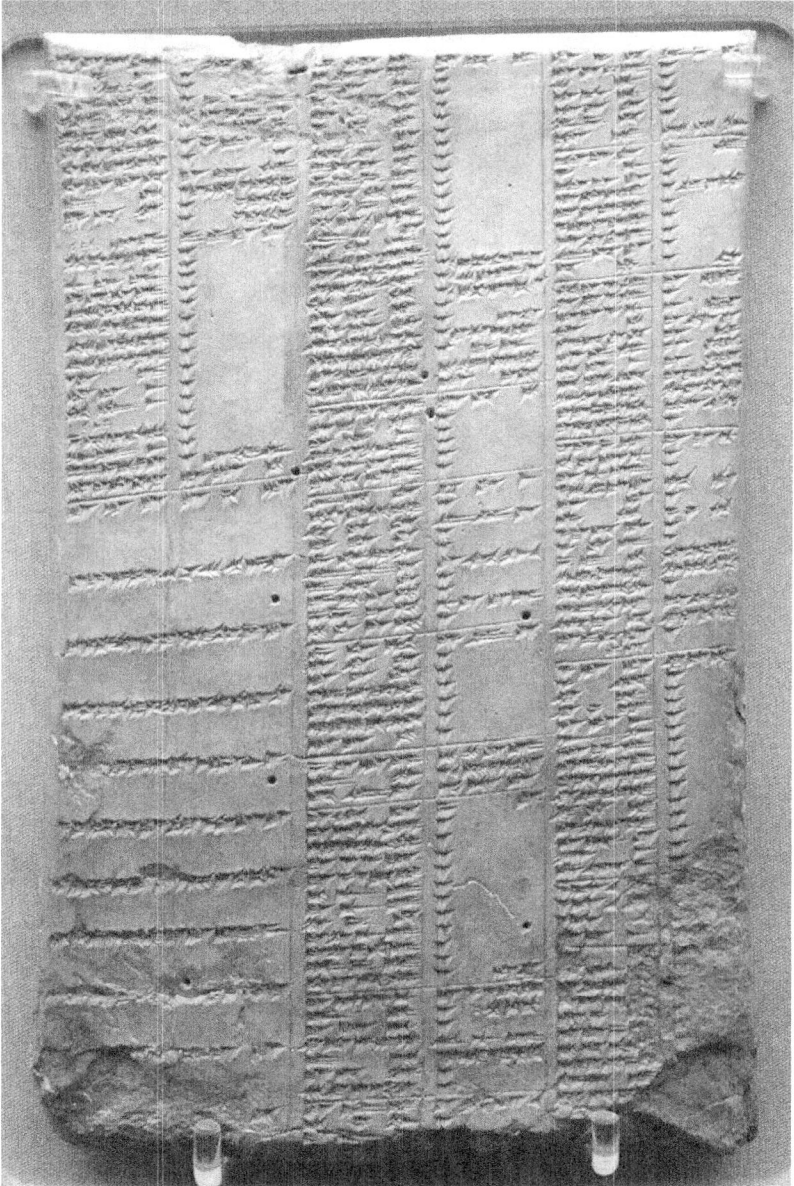

Illustration 37

Response: _____

8. Kings often wrote laws and other declarations on cuneiform tablets. However, this tablet has different royal rules. What rules could these be?

Illustration 38

Response:

_____

_____

_____

9. This figure depicts one of the few famous female scribes. Who was she?

Illustration 39

Response: _____

10. On this map is the city where over 30,000 clay tablets were discovered from the Assyrian Empire. Which city was this?

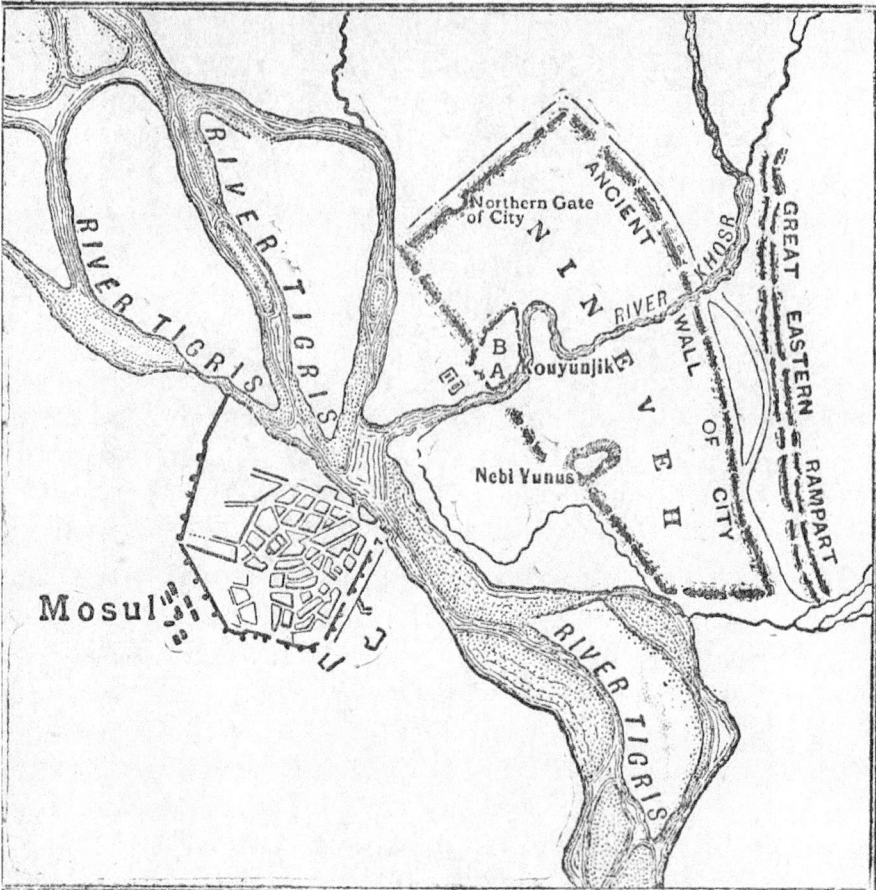

Illustration 40

Response: _____

Short Answer

1. Describe how the invention of writing transformed Mesopotamian society.

_____

_____

_____

2. Why did cuneiform writing help improve agriculture and other industries?

_____

_____

_____

3. Which came first, the simple marks or symbols representing sounds?

_____

_____

_____

4. Who helped young scribes learn their lessons?

_____

_____

_____

5. What were the main subjects young scribes were given to learn?

_____

_____

_____

6. Why are cuneiform tablets found in archaeological excavations (and the ones yet to be found) so important?

_____

_____

_____

7. Why was the early cuneiform so different from the later versions?

_____

_____

_____

8. When did cuneiform become more complex?

_____

_____

_____

9. With the introduction of writing, even the roles of some deities changed. Why?

_____

_____

_____

10. How did the number of characters change in cuneiform?

_____

_____

_____

Chapter 5: Empires Rise and Fall: Mesopotamian Kingdoms and Rulers

Like many other empires, the Mesopotamian kingdoms also saw many rulers rise and fall. Some were more liked, others not so much, but they still led their empire to triumph.

From Sargon of Akkad to Ashurbanipal, Mesopotamia had many strong kings. This chapter talks about their efforts and rule and the most significant events throughout the history of each empire and dynasty.

Some kings (for example, Gilgamesh) you may have heard of, but others may be less known. Make sure to read the questions carefully to learn the most about the rise and fall of the Mesopotamian empires and rulers.

Multiple Choice Questions

1. Who was the ruler famous for creating the first empire in Mesopotamia?

    A. Nebuchadnezzar II

    B. Sargon of Akkad

    C. Gilgamesh

    D. Hammurabi

2. Besides being a famous hero (known for his own Epic), Gilgamesh was also a...

    A. King

    B. Ruler of a city-state

    C. Priest

    D. God

3. Who was the sixth king of Babylon and the founder of the Babylonian Empire?

    A. Nebuchadnezzar

    B. Nabopolassar

    C. Hammurabi

    D. Naram-Sin

4. Which ruler aligned himself with the Medes to conquer Nineveh city and overthrow the Assyrian Empire?

    A. Hammurabi

    B. Nabopolassar

    C. Nebuchadnezzar

    D. Ashurbanipal

5. Who founded the first Assyrian Empire?

    A. Tiglath-Pileser III

    B. Sennacherib

    C. Ashurbanipal

    D. Shamshi-Adad I

6. Which Persian ruler is known for invading Greece?

    A. Xerxes I

    B. Cyrus the Great

    C. Darius II

    D. Darius I

7. Later on, the king shared his governing responsibilities with another very important person. Who was this person?

    A. The chief administrator

    B. The high priest

    C. The ruler of the city-states

    D. The queen

8. What contributed to wars the most in ancient times?

    A. Religion

    B. Trade

    C. Resources

    D. Climate

9. How many city-states were in the first Akkadian Empire?

    A. 55

    B. 45

    C. 65

    D. 75

10. Who caused the surprising downfall of the Akkadian Empire?

    A. The leaders of the latest rebellion

    B. Inadequate government

    C. Conflict between the king and the high priest

    D. The Gutians

True or False

1. The Code of Hammurabi is one of the oldest and longest-deciphered writings of the world.

- True
- False

2. The Akkadian Empire reached its peak during the reign of Sargon the Great.

- True
- False

3. North and South Mesopotamia were united for several millennia B.C.E.

- True
- False

4. Despite his efforts to make the Assyrian Empire powerful and culturally rich, Ashurbanipal did not succeed.

- True
- False

5. Cyrus the Great ruled the Persian Empire at its peak.

- True
- False

6. The Persian army suffered a loss in both Persian Wars.

- True
- False

7. The exiled Jews were later allowed to return to Jerusalem.

- True
- False

8. Kingship in Mesopotamia existed before the rise of the world's first empire.

- True
- False

9. Before the Akkadian Empire, the city-states were under the main king's rule.

- True
- False

10. The conquered city-states were satisfied with the Akkadian government.

- True
- False

Fill-in-the-Blank

1. The Assyrian Empire was known for its powerful army and excellent _____ skills.

2. Ruling from 2254 to 2218 B.C.E., Naram-Sin was Sargon's _____ and the first Mesopotamian ruler claiming to be a _____.

3. After conquering them, Nebuchadnezzar II sent the _____ into exile.

4. King Sennacherib conquered _____ and rebuilt the city of _____, turning it into one of the most stunning cities in ancient history.

5. The last truly powerful king of the Assyrian Empire was _____.

6. Sargon the Great claimed that his military success was due to guidance he received from the goddess _____.

7. One of the lesser-known inventions originating from Mesopotamia is the concept of _____.

8. The structure of the Mesopotamian government _____ with the rise and fall of the successive _____.

9. As the Mesopotamian rule expanded, it became impossible for one ruler to govern both the _____ and _____ duties.

10. The first war in Mesopotamia (and possibly in history) happened during the Second Early Dynastic II when _____ of Kish conquered _____ in 2700 B.C.E.

Picture-Based Questions

1. Which Mesopotamian empire built this iconic structure?

Illustration 41

Response:

_____

_____

_____

2. In Assyrian depictions like this, the status of a person could easily be determined. Can you guess what was the status of the person pictured here?

Illustration 42

Response:

_____

_____

_____

3. The list on this clay slab contains the names of all Sumerian cities, settlements, and their rulers. Do you know what this list is called?

Illustration 43

Response:

4. This tablet talks about the first ruler after the mythical Great Flood. What was the ruler's name?

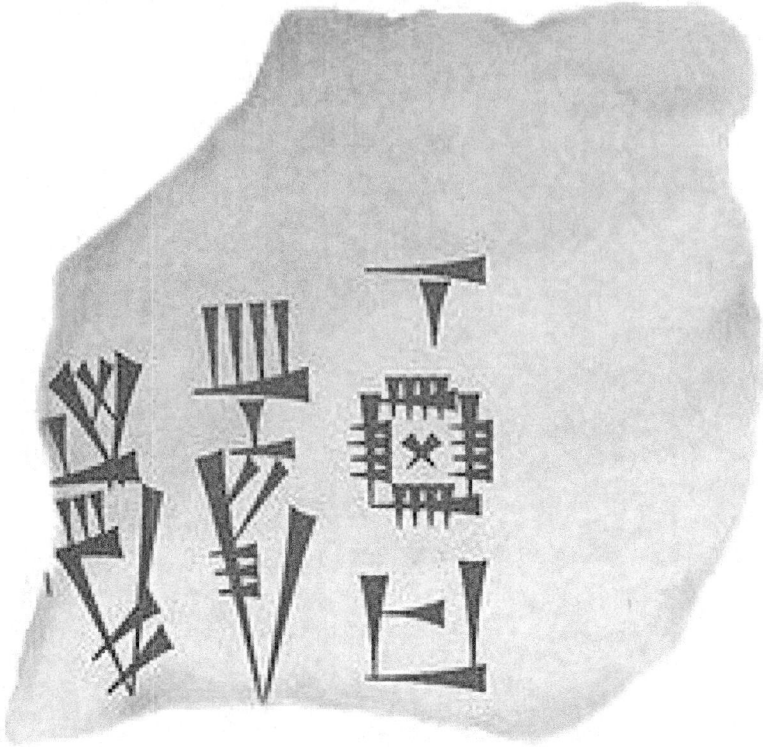

Illustration 44

Response:

_____

_____

_____

5. One of the city-states on this map was considered the oldest city in the world by the Sumerians. Which city was this?

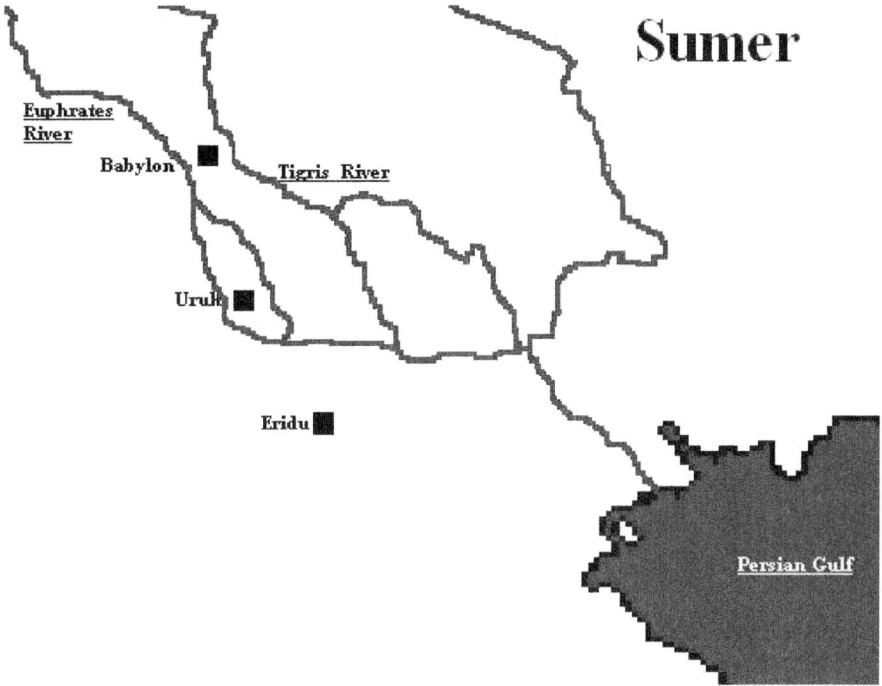

Illustration 45

Response:

_____

_____

_____

6. This map shows the major Lower Mesopotamian cities during the time when the Sumerian settlements founded during the Uruk period expanded, forcing the king to give up some of his power. What was the name of this period?

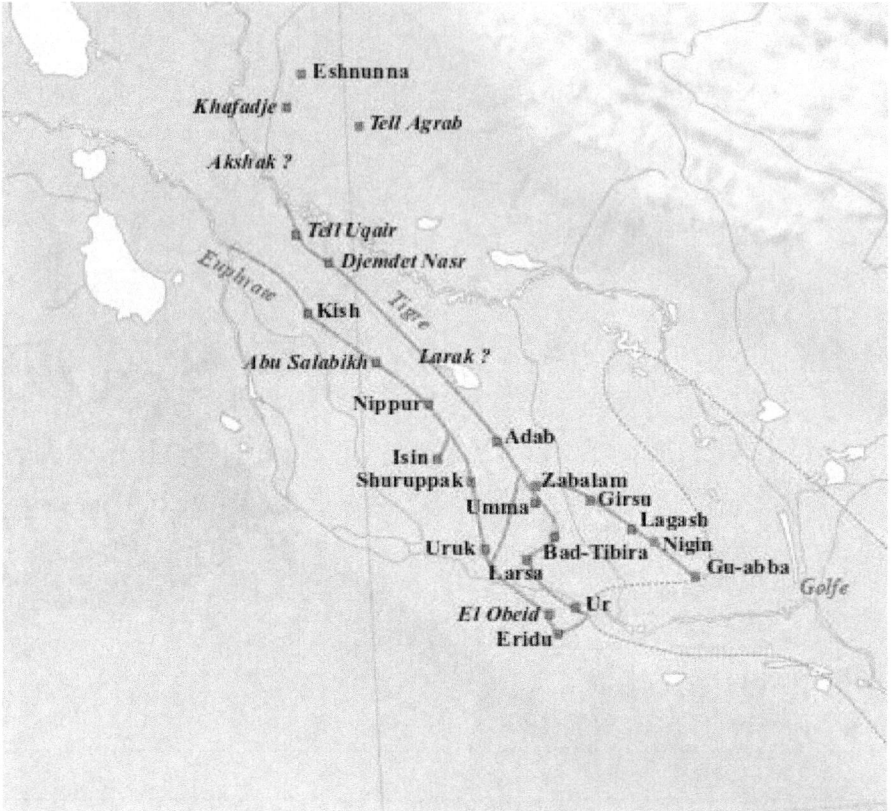

Illustration 46

Response:

_____

_____

_____

7. The neighboring territory highlighted in the middle was important in the history of Mesopotamian warfare. Why?

Illustration 47

Response:

_____

_____

_____

8. She was the only queen on the extensive Sumerian King List. What was her name?

Illustration 48

Response:

_____

_____

_____

9. The person seated on the throne in this picture was the patron of the Sumerian dynasty. Who was this person?

Illustration 49

Response:

_____

_____

_____

10. On the right is the deity who replaced many of the ancient Mesopotamian gods. On the left is the king of one of the last empires. What are their names?

Illustration 50

Response:

_____

_____

_____

Short Answer

1. What were some of the key achievements of the Babylonian Empire under Nebuchadnezzar II?

_____

_____

_____

2. Which ruler made the most advances in the Mesopotamian political and military system?

_____

_____

_____

3. How did Cyrus the Great save a Mesopotamian empire?

_____

_____

_____

4. What was the main concept the early Mesopotamian government was based on?

_____

_____

_____

5. What did Sargon of Akkad do immediately after conquering the Sumerian city-states?

_____

_____

_____

6. What was the advantage Ur-Nammu had over the previous rulers in Mesopotamia?

_____

_____

_____

7. What contributions did Shulgi of Ur, the son of Ur-Nammu, have on Mesopotamian politics and society?

_____

_____

_____

8. Besides a king and the founder of legal codes, what other names or titles were increased to Hammurabi?

_____

_____

_____

9. How did the Code of Hammurabi impact people's social status?

_____

_____

_____

10. How did religion shift during the succession of the empires?

_____

_____

_____

Chapter 6: Daily Life in Ancient Mesopotamia

Did you know that Mesopotamians lived very similarly to modern civilizations? Children went to school, most parents worked, families gathered for dinner, and their homes had furniture similar to what you would find in homes today.

Of course, there were differences in social classes and societal rules, but as you'll learn from this chapter, daily life in Mesopotamia was very colorful and eventful.

Multiple Choice Questions

1. What was the primary material used for building houses in ancient Mesopotamia?

   A. Wood

   B. Stone

   C. Mud-brick

   D. Reed

2. What did Mesopotamians do before agriculture became popular and the cities began to grow?

   A. Fish

   B. Hunting and gathering

   C. Moved to find food and resources

   D. Pillaged from neighboring villages

3. Who belonged to the middle class in Mesopotamian society?

    A. Craftsman, merchants, and civil servants

    B. Scribes and farmers

    C. Priestesses and laborers

    D. Traders and priests

4. What was Mesopotamian clothing made of?

    A. Textile

    B. Wool

    C. Sheepskin

    D. Other natural materials

5. What did daily life depend on for each person?

    A. Their social status and occupation

    B. Their place of birth

    C. Where they lived

    D. Their connection to the king

6. Why were kings so respected and honored in life and death?

    A. They were just

    B. They caused great fear

    C. They were seen as divine messengers

    D. They were thought to be gods

7. What was the role of the lesser priests and priestesses?

    A. Conveying messages between the people and the higher priests and priestesses

    B. Overseeing the sacred aspects of daily life in the temple complex

    C. Serving the kings and higher religious leaders

    D. Electing higher priests and priestesses

8. Who were the first doctors in ancient Mesopotamia?

    A. Priestesses

    B. Regular older women

    C. Older, wise men

    D. Scribes

9. Merchants were found in all social classes. What was the key difference between the lives of merchants in different classes?

    A. The amount of free time

    B. The social status

    C. The money they earned

    D. All of the above

10. What other titles did Mesopotamian teachers have?

    A. Tutor

    B. Scribe

    C. Administrator

    D. Priest

True or False

1. In ancient Mesopotamia, women were often scribes and scholars.

- True
- False

2. After the cities began to grow, people didn't want to work in agriculture anymore.

- True
- False

3. Laborers and farmers had a harder life, but their hard work often paid off.

- True
- False

4. The slaves were at the bottom of Mesopotamian society.

- True
- False

5. Art and poetry were a big part of city life in Mesopotamia.

- True
- False

6. Men and women had long hair.

- True
- False

7. Everyone had access to candles for lighting.

- True
- False

8. Only adults could be slaves in ancient Mesopotamia.

- True
- False

9. Perfume makers could easily rise from a lower class to an upper level in society.

- True
- False

10. During the Akkadian Empire, all Mesopotamians lived under a unified rule and empire.

- True
- False

Fill-in-the-Blank

1. Mesopotamians used _____ as a form of currency in their trade and economic transactions.

2. When the cities grew, more people were able to get a _____ because there were a lot more duties and _____ to do.

3. Mesopotamian societies were divided into different _____ of people.

4. The top of the Mesopotamian hierarchy was occupied by the _____.

5. The upper level of Mesopotamian society was made up of wealthy members, like _____, _____, and high-level _____.

6. Laborers and farmers belonged to the _____ class.

7. Besides work, people in the larger towns and cities also found the opportunity for _____ _____.

8. Both women and men wore _____, especially in the upper classes.

9. Wealthier homes had _____ to let in more _____ and sesame oil _____ for additional lighting.

10. Ancient Mesopotamians would _____ and _____ in clean clothes for the evening meal.

Picture-Based Questions

1. Describe what activities might be taking place in this marketplace.

Illustration 51

Response:

_____

_____

_____

2. What important part of Mesopotamian social life is shown in this picture?

Illustration 52

Response:

_____

_____

_____

3. What was the purpose of this object in daily life in ancient Mesopotamia?

Illustration 53

Response:

_____

_____

_____

4. What social event could be shown on this relief, and who is participating?

Illustration 54

Response:

_____

_____

_____

5. This tablet shows people from the Neo-Babylonian Empire. Notice anything interesting about them?

Illustration 55

Response:

_____

_____

_____

6. This object often appeared in wealthy Assyrian households. Do you know its purpose?

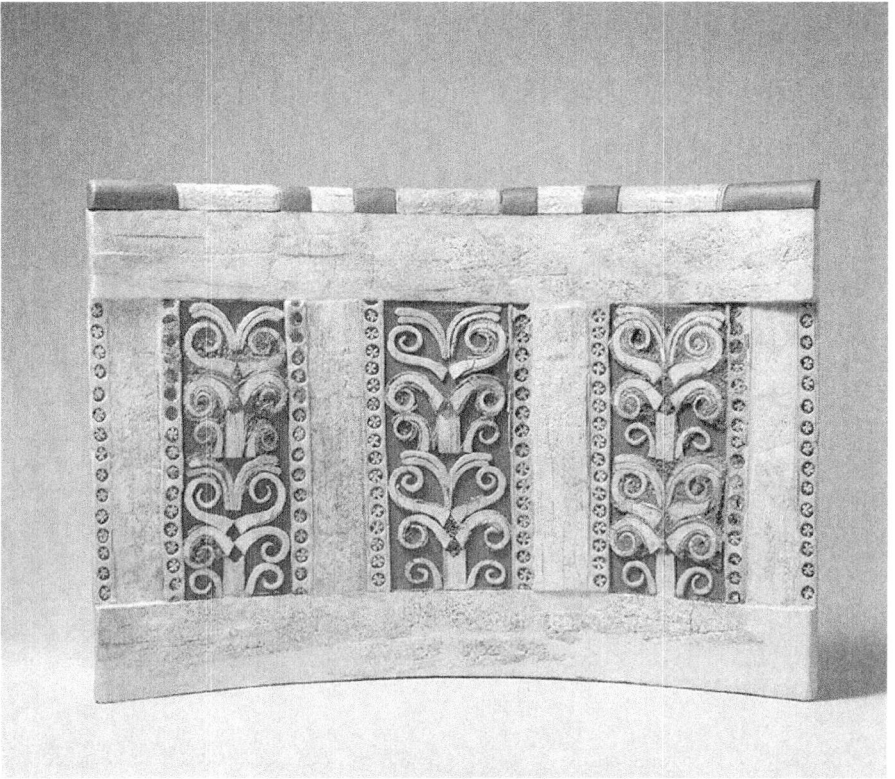

Illustration 56

Response:

_____

_____

_____

7. Workers like the one on the right side of the picture were essential for keeping the city working. What were their roles?

Illustration 57

Response:

_____

_____

_____

8. This Sumerian queen is the perfect example of how people could rise in the ranks in ancient Mesopotamia. Who was she?

Illustration 58

Response:

_____

_____

_____

9. This goddess had a jump rump game named after her in ancient Mesopotamia. What was her name?

Illustration 59

Response:

_____

_____

_____

10. This plaque shows two people drinking in ancient Mesopotamia. What do you think was their drink of choice?

Illustration 60

Response:

_____

_____

_____

Short Answer

1. What kind of jobs did the Mesopotamians have in the cities?

_____

_____

_____

2. Why did Mesopotamians rely on trade to advance their societies?

_____

_____

_____

3. How did the Mesopotamians contribute to advances in agriculture?

_____

_____

_____

4. What did Mesopotamian homes look like?

_____

_____

_____

5. What did the ancient Mesopotamians do for fun?

_____

_____

_____

6. What did a typical meal look like in a Mesopotamian home?

_____

_____

_____

7. What kind of furniture did the Mesopotamian homes have?

_____

_____

_____

8. What did children play with?

_____

_____

_____

9. Why was writing so important for the Mesopotamians?

_____

_____

_____

10. How did wealthy families ensure their children get the best education?

_____

_____

_____

At Home in Mesopotamia: Family and Daily Life

The typical Mesopotamian family had a father, a mother, children, and sometimes other family members. The father was the head of the household, and everyone, including the mother and the children, had to obey him.

Most people begin their days early, with women rising first to prepare breakfast (in wealthier homes, this was the slaves' job). They would usually prepare two meals a day, one before the start of the workday (breakfast) and one after the workday ended (dinner).

Throughout the day, women continued to take care of their home and their family. Some women worked as tavern keepers, potters, or weavers. Those who worked outside the home most of the day (both men and women) would take a piece of bread as a midday snack with them.

Wealthier families sent their sons to school while the daughters learned how to run a household. In poor families, sons and daughters all worked around the house, either with the mother or father.

In wealthier families, only the father worked. Midday, they would go to a city tavern with his friends and have a meal washed down by a cup of beer. Poor people only went home for dinner when all family members would gather and get ready to spend time together.

By dinner, children arrived home from school, or they were done with their chores and perhaps even played a little with their friends. After dinner, they would sit with the parents and listen to their stories or play music or games together.

Chapter 7: Architects and Builders: Mesopotamian Innovations

The great ziggurats and the complex irrigation system were only two of the architectural marvels originating from ancient Mesopotamia. The empires were marked by remarkable building innovations and solutions that not only benefited the city but also the growth of the entire civilization.

In this chapter, you can test your knowledge of Mesopotamian architecture and see how it shaped the progress of early human civilizations. As always, you'll also find an addition with a peak into a unique aspect of the chapter's topic – in this case, interesting facts about some of the most famous Mesopotamian structures and innovative solutions.

Multiple Choice:

1. The ziggurat was primarily used as a:

    A. Royal Palace

    B. Marketplace

    C. Religious temple

    D. Gathering place for public events

2. **What was unique about the first places of worship in Mesopotamia?**

    A. Nature motifs

    B. Depiction of gods and goddesses

    C. Pictures of people

    D. The shape of the buildings

3. **Which structures were built around the cities in the Uruk Period (before the first dynasty)?**

    A. Temples

    B. Walls with watchtowers

    C. Gates

    D. Gardens

4. **Besides the cities, which other structures had their own walls?**

    A. Temples

    B. Royal courts and palaces

    C. Administrator houses

    D. Schools

5. **When did anthropomorphic (man-like) figures start to appear in building decorations?**

    A. In the Akkadian Empire

    B. In the Assyrian Empire

    C. During the Third Dynasty of Ur

    D. During the Neo-Assyrian period

6. **Which ruler built one of Mesopotamia's most famous remaining architectural structures in 575 B.C.E.?**

    A. Nebuchadnezzar II

    B. Nebuchadnezzar

    C. Ashurbanipal

    D. Ashurbanipal II

7. What principle were most Mesopotamian architects and builders driven by?

  A. Closeness to nature

  B. Mirroring nature

  C. Opposing nature

  D. Disregarding nature

8. What were the key elements of Mesopotamian architecture?

  A. Complex irrigation systems

  B. Ziggurats

  C. Mud brick buildings decorated with carvings, reliefs, and other intricate elements

  D. All of the above

9. The building of never-before-seen structures and solutions required skills, courage, and what else?

  A. Imagination and thinking outside the box

  B. Looking into other civilizations' techniques

  C. Years of studying

  D. Learning to create more practical objects

10. Which famous Babylonian structure is known only from myths and religious texts?

  A. The Hanging Gardens of Babylon

  B. The Tower of Babel

  C. The Ziggurat of Ur

  D. The Ishtar Gate

True or False

1. Mesopotamian cities were among the first to implement a grid layout for city streets.

  - True

  - False

2. The purpose of the first larger buildings in Mesopotamian settlements was worship.

  - True

  - False

3. Between 5000 and 4100 B.C.E., the Mesopotamians built only mud-brick houses and buildings.

- True
- False

4. The first canals and aqueducts for irrigation were built after the formation of the Akkadian Empire.

- True
- False

5. Art and architecture began to thrive even more after the kingship and priesthood were divided.

- True
- False

6. Ur-Nammu completed the building of the Great Ziggurat of Ur by 2030 B.C.E.

- True
- False

7. The last Babylonian king made great efforts to restore the architectural wonders of previous empires.

- True
- False.

8. Ziggurats were sometimes used for political events, too.

- True
- False

9. There were other large gardens built before the Hanging Gardens of Babylon.

- True
- False

10. Decorative elements and furniture found in the ruins of Uruk indicate they were created in honor of Ea.

- True
- False

Fill-in-the-Blank

1. The _____ system was a key innovation that allowed Mesopotamians to control river water for irrigation.

2. The earliest temples had _____ buildings laid out in a _____ pattern and _____ pillars.

3. The Mesopotamians perfected the construction of ziggurats in the _____ period.

4. _____ and _____ made some of Mesopotamia's most memorable works during the height of the Akkadian Empire.

5. Ur-Nammu built palaces and courts surrounded by _____ and _____.

6. Shulgi of Ur continued his father's legacy by founding the first _____ _____ with landscaped gardens.

7. Besides making the buildings look nicer, the intricate decorations on Mesopotamian buildings also showcased political, religious, and _____ ideas.

8. Like many other places of worship in Mesopotamia, the Ziggurat of Ur has several _____ and is over 90 feet tall.

9. With its complex _____ and colorful _____, Babylonian architecture art was a true representation of the civilization's cultural and monetary riches.

10. Since most other large Mesopotamian gardens were all built near large _____, where there were walls, shade, and sufficient water resources, some believe that the Hanging Gardens of Babylon may have been built near the _____ of Nebuchadnezzar.

Picture-Based Questions

1. Identify this structure and its likely purpose in Mesopotamian society.

Illustration 61

Response:

_____

_____

_____

2. What Mesopotamian invention is tied to the settlement shown on the map?

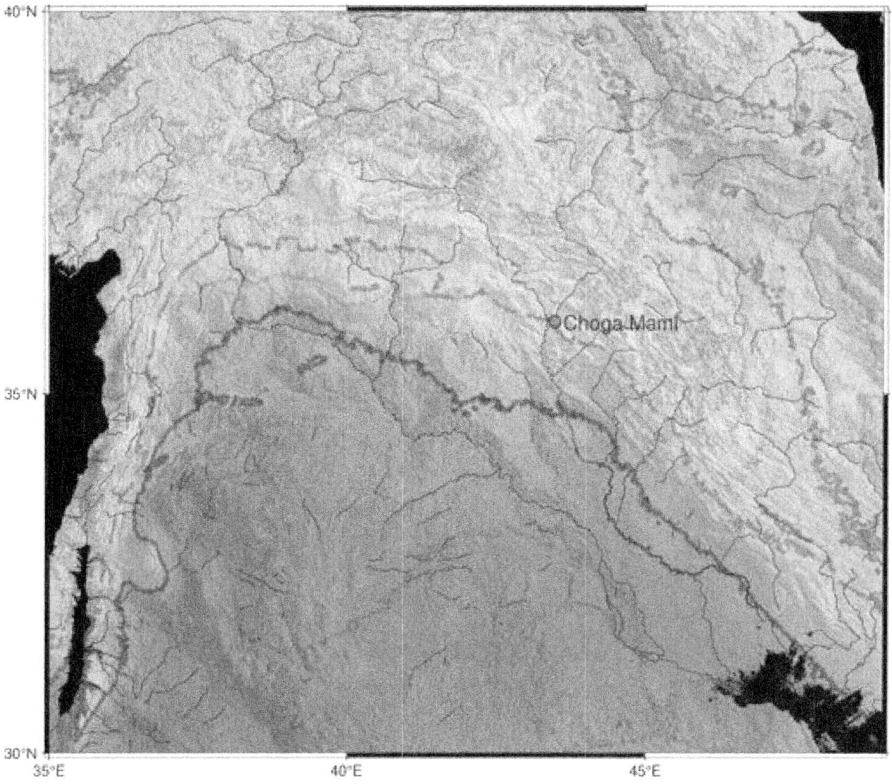

Illustration 62

Response: _____

3. Plaques like this were common decorations in middle- to upper-class homes, but they also had other purposes. What do you think their purpose was?

Illustration 63

Response:

_____

_____

_____

4. What do you think this tool was used for in Mesopotamian architecture?

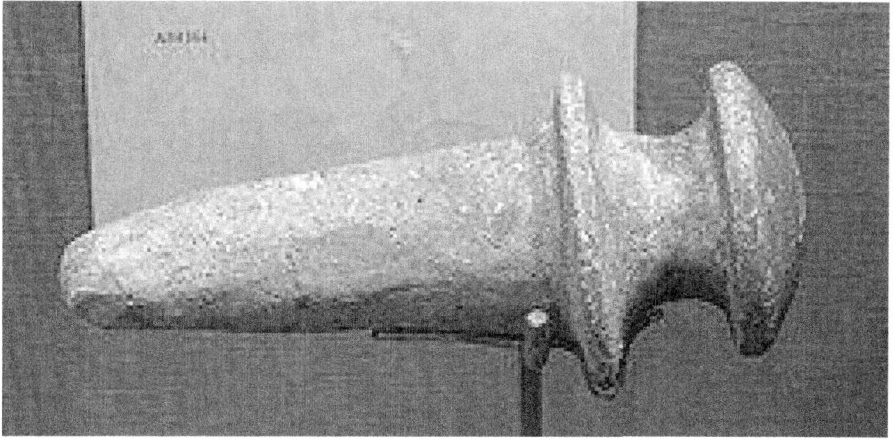

Illustration 64

Response:

_____

_____

_____

5. Early Mesopotamian art and architecture had a few common themes. What was the theme for these art pieces?

Illustration 65

Response: _____

6. Where was this object used?

Illustration 66

Response:

_____

_____

_____

7. Which mythical Mesopotamian architectural innovation is supposed to be located at this site?

Illustration 67

Response: _____

8. These decorative-looking pegs were not actually used for decoration. Can you guess their purpose?

Illustration 68

Response:

_____

_____

_____

9. Name this ziggurat. Hint: It was partially destroyed by King Ashurbanipal in 640 B.C.E.

Illustration 69

Response: _____

10. To which ancient settlement do these ruins belong?

Illustration 70

Response: _____

Short Answer

1. Discuss the significance of the Hanging Gardens of Babylon in Mesopotamian architecture and culture.

2. What are the examples of early Mesopotamian artwork?

3. What did Mesopotamian places look like by the early 21st century B.C.E.?

4. Describe all the factors Mesopotamian architecture considered when building something.

5. What was the Mesopotamians' first move in establishing a better irrigation system?

6. What made the construction of temples different from the building of regular homes?

_____

_____

_____

7. What did the successful completion of a structure mean for the builders, architects, and other artists working on it?

_____

_____

_____

8. What did Mesopotamians do before the final completion of a building?

_____

_____

_____

9. Why were Mesopotamian rulers pictured with or alongside religious motifs in architectural decorations?

_____

_____

_____

10. Which unique decoration carving techniques did the Assyrians develop?

_____

_____

_____

Chapter 8: Warriors and Conquerors: Military History of Mesopotamia

The military history of Mesopotamia began with small conflicts among Sumerian settlements and evolved into the courageous acts of the Akkadian, Babylonian, Assyrian, and Persian rulers.

This chapter will introduce you to common strategies, important battles, and heroic leaders that shaped Mesopotamian history. You'll be reading about surprising military and diplomatic maneuvers, along with interesting facts about the greatest leaders and conquerors.

Multiple Choice Questions

1. Which Mesopotamian ruler is known for creating one of the world's first empires through military conquest?

   A. Gilgamesh

   B. Nebuchadnezzar

   C. Sargon of Akkad

   D. Nebuchadnezzar II

2. Imperialism was thriving in which Mesopotamian area?

    A. North

    B. South

    C. Central

    D. Riverside

3. When did the Stele of the Vultures monument celebrate victory over Umma?

    A. 2700 B.C.E.

    B. 2500 B.C.E.

    C. 2300 B.C.E.

    D. 2600 B.C.E.

4. Besides maintaining natural order, Eannatum also had other intentions when attacking Umma. What was it?

    A. Avenging a transgression

    B. Gathering resources

    C. Conquering lands

    D. Gaining control of the trade routes

5. In freshly conquered cities in the Akkadian Empire, there were always armed warriors patrolling the streets. Why?

    A. For safety reasons

    B. The king didn't trust people's loyalty

    C. To cause fear

    D. To solidify power

6. What was the most significant improvement in Mesopotamian warfare?

    A. A unique attack strategy

    B. Better defense strategy

    C. The composite bow

    D. The training method

7. A new weapon meant removing another tool from the front line. Which tool was it?

    A. Shields

    B. Armories

    C. Chariots

    D. Lookout posts

8. Which king took control over the Assyrian territories by conquering the Kingdom of Mitanni?

    A. Adad Nirari I

    B. Suppiluliuma I

    C. Tiglath Pileser I

    D. Ashurnasirpal II

9. Who was Tukulti-Ninurta I, and what was he known for?

    A. The Assyrian ruler who defeated the Hittites at the Battle of Nihriya

    B. The Assyrian ruler who conquered Babylon

    C. Receiving punishment for filling the treasury with Babylonian riches

    D. All of the above

10. What type of warfare did the Assyrians prefer?

    A. Defense

    B. Offense

    C. Siege

    D. Direct

True or False

1. The Assyrian army was known for its use of war elephants.

- True
- False

2. The first war in recorded history was the first true conflict in the world.

- True
- False

3. Mesopotamian geography was a common cause of wars.

- True
- False

4. According to some sources, warfare was a constant way of life in Mesopotamia.

- True
- False

5. In the early days of warfare, Mesopotamians did not use any special protective headgear in battles.

- True
- False

6. In the Akkadian Empire, the administrators were loyal to the king of the empire, not to the citizens.

- True
- False

7. Sometimes, the invention of defensive and offensive tactics and weaponry quickly followed each other.

- True
- False

8. Troops traveled with scribes whose only role was to record the events from the battlefield.

- True
- False

9. All kings of the Ur Period used the same ruling and conquering tactics.

- True
- False

10. The great Assyrian Empire, which Ashurnasirpal II took over, was partially built on stolen wealth.

- True
- False

Fill-in-the-Blank

1. The Battle of _____ was a significant conflict in Mesopotamian history involving the Babylonians and the Elamites.

2. In ancient Mesopotamia, armed conflicts were often recorded through _____ and cuneiform _____.

3. Sometimes, wars were fought not between two nations but between their _____ _____.

4. When several city-states or an empire went to a battle, each city-state had its own _____, which made organizing the strategy and _____ much easier.

5. To maintain order, Sargon and his successors installed trusted _____ and _____ _____ in important functions in all city-states.

6. People captured in battle could be executed, but also _____ or sometimes_____ after a time.

7. The Akkadian Empire declined and was defeated by the _____, who were then not only conquered but also _____ from Mesopotamia during the third Ur Period.

8. Hammurabi's empire was short-lived, but its conquerors, the _____, didn't have much batter either.

9. After the defeat of the Kassites, Mesopotamia went from one ruling power to another, beginning with the _____ and followed by a series of _____ powers.

10. During a siege, the Assyrians used _____ _____ to get in and take control of a city.

Picture-Based Question

1. Describe the warfare technique depicted in this relief.

Illustration 71

Response:

_____

_____

_____

2. The king on this relief is performing a common pre-battle ritual. Who was he, and what was he doing?

Illustration 72

Response:

_____

_____

_____

_____

3. This seal was issued by a king who was inspired and guided by several deities. What was his name?

Illustration 73

Response:

_____

_____

_____

4. Which category did this war chariot belong to, small or heavy?

Illustration 74

Response:

_____

_____

_____

5. What does this picture tell you about the Akkadian Empire and its rulers?

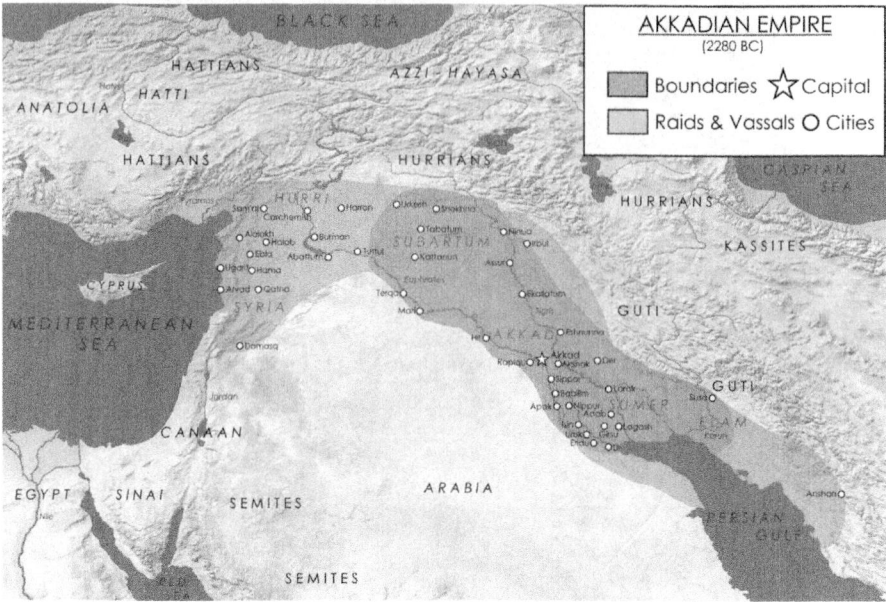

Illustration 75

Response:

_____

_____

_____

6. What was this object used for in Mesopotamian warfare?

Illustration 76

Response:

_____

_____

_____

7. At one point in time, the civilization highlighted on the map was much stronger than a Mesopotamian civilization. Yet, their conflict ended with an unexpected result. What was this result?

The Kingdom of Urartu, 9th-6th Centuries B.C.

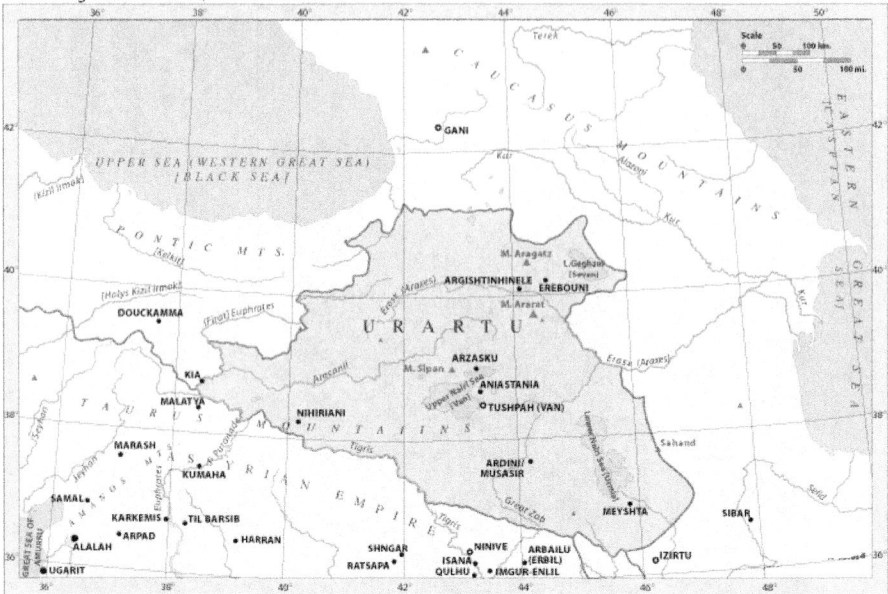

Illustration 77

Response:

_____

_____

_____

8. These members of the Assyrian militia were the most significant part of the infantry. Why?

Illustration 78

Response:

_____

_____

_____

9. This Assyrian king was known to do whatever it took to win a military campaign. Who was he?

Illustration 79

Response:

_____

_____

_____

10. Name this warrior king.

Hint: He ruled from Nineveh and never rebuilt a city he conquered and destroyed.

Illustration 80

Response:

_____

_____

_____

Short Answer

1. Explain the role of the chariot in Mesopotamian warfare.

_____

_____

_____

2. How did Mesopotamians use religion in warfare?

_____

_____

_____

3. What kind of weapons did Sumerians carry to battles?

_____

_____

_____

4. How did Sargon of Akkad improve the Mesopotamian military strategy?

_____

_____

_____

5. What allowed the Assyrians, led by Adad Nirari I, to establish the Assyrian Empire?

_____

_____

_____

6. Describe the pride of the Assyrian siege strategy, the battle engine.

_____

_____

_____

7. Like the Sumerians, Akkadians, and Babylonians before, the Assyrians continued to claim that conflicts were the gods' will. However, their methods of convincing people were somewhat different. Why?

_____

_____

_____

8. Which Mesopotamian king took no credit for his victories?

_____

_____

_____

9. Did the Persian kings rely on the same military tactics as their predecessors?

_____

_____

_____

10. According to a myth, Hammurabi's empire failed to survive for a very unusual reason. What was the reason?

_____

_____

_____

Chapter 9: Trade and Economy: The Bazaar of the Ancient World

Naturally, the fertile land of Mesopotamia, combined with the incredible skills of its inhabitants, soon led to a state where the settlements were producing more than needed. They had more fish, vegetables, fruits, meat, dairy, and nuts than they could consume. Yet they didn't have wood to build homes and shelters or metals to make weapons – but these were available in other lands.

As always, the Mesopotamians thought to make the best of the situation, and they started exchanging what they had for what others offered. This chapter will guide you through ancient trading routes, barter systems, and economic practices that connected Mesopotamia with other civilizations.

Multiple Choice Questions

1. Which of the following was a major trade commodity in ancient Mesopotamia?

   A. Silk

   B. Spices

   C. Wool

   D. Textile

2. What were outposts used for?

    A. Local trade

    B. Long-distance trade

    C. Inter-city trade

    D. Recording sales

3. What trading commodities were produced in temple workshops?

    A. Pottery and baskets

    B. Leather products and jewelry

    C. Devotional figurines and ivory carvings

    D. All of the above

4. Besides agricultural products, what other food items were exported from Mesopotamia?

    A. Dates

    B. Flax

    C. Rice

    D. Fish

5. Which Mesopotamian inventions helped improve trading?

    A. Mass production

    B. Writing

    C. Wheels

    D. Sails

6. Besides agriculture and food items, what other resources could Mesopotamia trade?

    A. Metals

    B. Construction material

    C. Papyrus

    D. Ivory

7. Which king improved Mesopotamian infrastructure, making overland trading easier?

    A. Hammurabi

    B. Shulgi

    C. Ur-Nammu

    D. Utu-Hegal

8. When did local trade begin in Mesopotamia?

    A. In the Uruk Period

    B. In the Ubaid Period

    C. In the first Empire

    D. In the Gutian Period

9. When did the Mesopotamians establish trade with Egypt?

    A. In the Ubaid period

    B. Before the Ubaid period

    C. In the Ur III period

    D. In the Uruk period

10. What role did ziggurats play in trading?

    A. Trading place

    B. Signal post

    C. Landmark

    D. Outposts

True or False

1. Mesopotamians used a barter system for most of their trading activities.

   - True
   - False

2. The Assyrian merchants were often family businesses trading locally in Mesopotamia and beyond.

   - True
   - False

3. The Assyrian merchants only traded local products.

   - True
   - False

4. Mesopotamian merchants began trading by establishing trade routes alongside the Tigris and the Euphrates rivers.

   - True
   - False

5. Mesopotamia started trading in all directions only in the first millennia.

   - True
   - False

6. Most long-distance trade was carried out on water routes.

   - True
   - False

7. Mesopotamia had resources for most essential goods.

   - True
   - False

8. Social revolts affected the Akkadian economic growth.

   - True
   - False

9. Mesopotamia showed a significant decline in trade during the Gutian Period.

   - True
   - False

10. At the turn of the 2nd millennium B.C.E., the revival of trade led to the Sumerian Renaissance

    - True
    - False

Fill-in-the-Blank

1. The city of _____ was a major trading hub in ancient Mesopotamia.

2. By the time of the Assyrian Empire, Mesopotamia was _____ grains, textiles, pottery, cooking oil, jewelry, leather goods, and baskets, and was _____ gold from Egypt, tin from Peris, silver from Anatolia, pears and ivory from India, and copper from Arabia.

3. Overland trade routes went _____ toward the Zagros Mountains and all the way to present-day Afghanistan and Iran.

4. The Sea route extended through the _____ across the _____ to the _____ in what is today's northern India and Pakistan.

5. Merchants and traders in early Mesopotamian cities began to form _____ for long-distance trading.

6. _____ and _____, used to make _____, were especially important imports from foreign lands.

7. In the early days, merchants traveled on _____ or used _____ to transport the goods.

8. Establishing trade routes to Egypt gave Mesopotamians access to imported _____ and the novelty item, _____.

9. During the Early Dynastic III period and up to 2334 B.C.E., _____ and _____ were the most dominant political and commercial powers.

10. A period of _____ during the Gutian period halted the trade because it took away the _____ surplus that was used for trading.

Picture-Based Question

1. What was the primary use of these seals in Mesopotamian trade?

Illustration 81

Response:

_____

_____

_____

2. This clay tablet records the trade of silver and textiles between Assyrian merchants and one of their main trading associates. Who were these associates?

Illustration 82

Response:

_____

_____

_____

3. Mesopotamians loved wearing jewelry just as much as they liked exporting it. However, doing both depended on trade. Why? Hint: Take a look at the picture to find the answer.

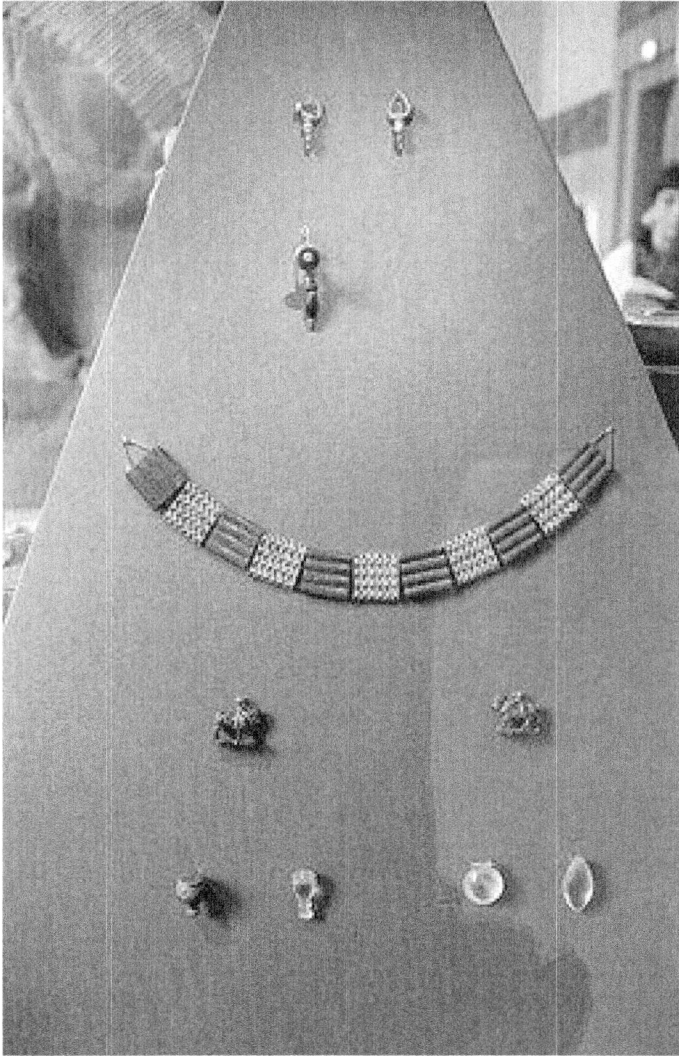

Illustration 83

Response:

_____

_____

_____

4. This was the first standardized coin used in trade in Mesopotamia. Who introduced it?

Illustration 84

Response:

_____

_____

_____

5. What were these clay tokens used for in trade?

Illustration 85

Response:

_____

_____

_____

6. This is one of the letters between Egypt and the Club of Great Powers, which talks about the thriving trade system between the civilizations. What's the name of the letters?

Illustration 86

Response: _____

7. Which of the larger cities on this map (marked with red letters) was a central spot for trading with the Indus Valley civilization?

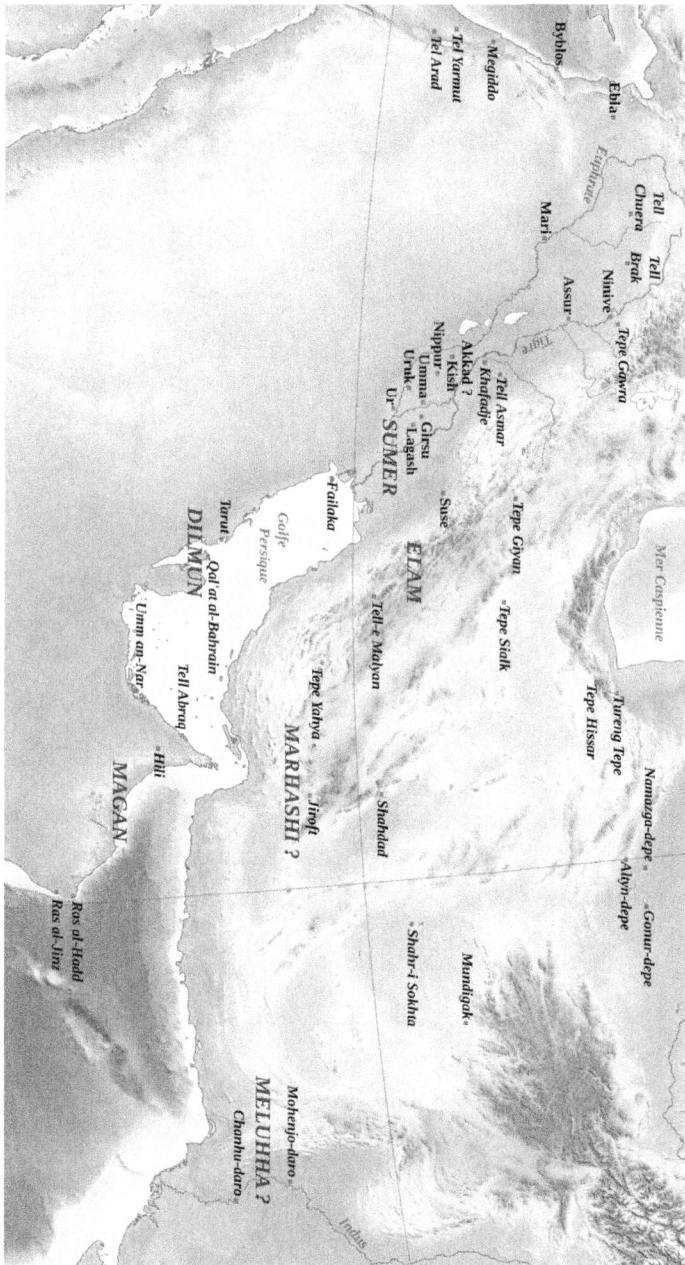

Illustration 87

Response: _____

8. When was trading these figurines popular in Mesopotamia?

Illustration 88

Response: _____

9. This map highlights an early trade route, which was later abandoned. In which direction did this route go?

Illustration 89

Response: _____

10. While Mesopotamians exported lots of finished metal products, these were used for different purposes. What was their purpose?

Illustration 90

Response:

_____

_____

_____

Short Answer

1. Discuss the importance of the Tigris and Euphrates rivers in Mesopotamian trade.

_____

_____

_____

2. How did long-distance trade work in ancient times?

_____

_____

_____

3. What was the benefit of local and long-distance trade, respectively?

_____

_____

_____

4. What tools did the Mesopotamians use to transport goods?

_____

_____

_____

5. What made overland trading difficult for merchants?

_____

_____

_____

6. Local and long-distance trade flourished under Akkadian rule. Why?

_____

_____

_____

7. How did Shulgi of Ur uplift trading again after the Gutian period?

_____

_____

_____

8. Why was Hammurabi's rule important for Mesopotamian trading?

_____

_____

_____

9. Who was the Club of the Great Powers, and what was its role?

_____

_____

_____

10. Some believe that the barter system led to the invention of cuneiform writing. Why and how do you think this could've happened?

_____

_____

_____

Chapter 10: Mesopotamia's Legacy and Influence on the Modern World

Its history may be thousands of years old, but Mesopotamia undoubtedly had a massive influence on the modern world. Mesopotamian inventions, innovative solutions, and findings either shaped the evolution of modern ideas of science and daily living or became part of these.

The modern law, where the presumption of innocence is a given fact, and the contemporary astronomical findings are tied to later Mesopotamian findings. Going back to the early days, the irrigation system or the script that gave way to ideas was a stepping stone leading to the evolution of modern societies.

The above examples are just a few ways Mesopotamia impacted modern civilizations. In this chapter, you can test your knowledge of contemporary Mesopotamian influences in science, art, architecture, and more.

Multiple Choice

1. Which modern mathematical concept originated in ancient Mesopotamia?

    A. The concept of zero

    B. The 60-minute hour

    C. Algebra

    D. Accounting

2. Which Mesopotamian calendar influenced modern calendars?

    A. Babylonian

    B. Lunar

    C. Pentecostal calendar

    D. Umma calendar

3. Which modern mathematical discipline was influenced the most by Mesopotamian scientific discoveries?

    A. Topology

    B. Algebra

    C. Geometry

    D. Arithmetic

4. What Mesopotamian invention created the foundation for stable settlements and societies?

    A. Writing

    B. Irrigation

    C. Transportation systems

    D. Money

5. Besides necessary resources, what else did the Mesopotamians trade with their neighbors?

    A. Experience

    B. Skilled workers

    C. Slaves

    D. Technological solutions

6. Which Mesopotamian invention laid the groundwork for modern monetary systems?

    A. Money

    B. Barter system

    C. Standardized weights and measures

    D. Standardized trading rules

7. Which Mesopotamian invention revolutionized trade and transportation across the world?

    A. Water trade

    B. Overland trade

    C. Chariots

    D. Wheel

8. The Mesopotamian approach to health was forgotten throughout history but has made a comeback in the last century. What's the name of this approach?

    A. Natural healing

    B. Holistic healing

    C. Herbal healing

    D. Transformative healing

9. What very modern problems did Mesopotamians face and resolve in their urban environments?

    A. Congestion

    B. Waste management

    C. Resource dispersion

    D. Crime

10. Which Mesopotamian invention transformed warfare?

    A. Wheel

    B. Composite bow

    C. Metal helmets

    D. Battle ax

True or False

1. The Mesopotamian base-60 number system is still used today in measuring time and angles.

   - True

   - False

2. Cuneiform writing had a significant influence on communication methods.

   - True

   - False

3. Mesopotamians weren't skilled astronomers.

   - True

   - False

4. Mesopotamian architecture inspired modern art and architectural design.

   - True

   - False

5. Mesopotamian art didn't have much impact on modern cultures.

   - True

   - False

6. Mesopotamian myths and tales contain very little cues about the ancient world.

   - True

   - False

7. Mesopotamia was one of the first civilizations to develop a trade system beyond its borders.

   - True

   - False

8. Mesopotamian governance was completely monarchical.

   - True

   - False

9. Mesopotamian urban planning focused on sustainability and efficient use of available resources.

- True
- False

10. In ancient times, Mesopotamia was a major center of learning and education.

- True
- False

Fill-in-the-Blank

1. The _____ Code, one of the oldest law codes, influenced modern legal systems.

2. The _____ still influences contemporary literature and storytelling.

3. Mesopotamians made significant advances in the fields of _____, which have impacted modern disciplines.

4. Modern agriculture uses similar _____ systems and _____ as did the Mesopotamians on the fields between the Tigris and the Euphrates.

5. The _____ alphabet, which evolved from the _____ script, was the prototype of the alphabets used in many languages today.

6. Many biblical tales, like the story of the _____, have parallels in Mesopotamian lore, reflecting shared cultural values.

7. The concept of the _____ _____, where life is regulated by _____, can be traced back to the Mesopotamian civilization.

8. Many principles of ancient Mesopotamian medicine, including the _____ process and the use of _____ _____, can be found in modern healthcare practices.

9. Mesopotamia's development of urban infrastructure, canals, buildings, roads, and trade routes are early examples of _____ _____.

10. The power of _____ was another Mesopotamian legacy for modern societies.

Picture-Based Questions

1. Identify the Mesopotamian architectural influence in this modern structure.

Illustration 91

Response:

_____

_____

_____

2. Was this Mesopotamian number system used before or after the invention of zero?

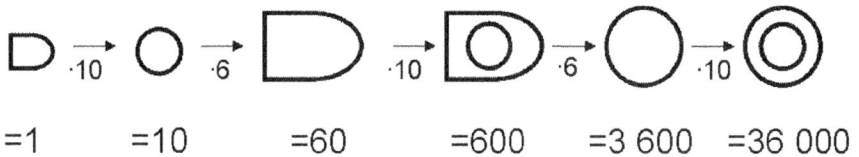

Illustration 92

Response:

_____

_____

_____

3. The paintings on this pot are related to an ancient story that was originally titled He Who Saw the Deep. What's the modern name of this story?

Illustration 93

Response:

_____

_____

_____

4. What do you think this modern painter was inspired by?

Illustration 94

Response:

_____

_____

_____

5. Name this artist inspired by ancient Mesopotamian art.

Illustration 95

Response:

_____

_____

_____

6. Name this ancient religious dictionary that influenced many subsequent religious ideas, texts, and cultures.

Illustration 96

Response:

_____

_____

_____

7. Creatures like this often appear in modern art – from pictures to jewelry to decorations. Where else did they appear?

Illustration 97

Response:

_____

_____

_____

_____

8. Which constellation was identified by the Mesopotamians?

Illustration 98

Response:

_____

_____

_____

9. This picture shows the basic workings of a modern deep well used in agriculture. What was the inspiration for this system?

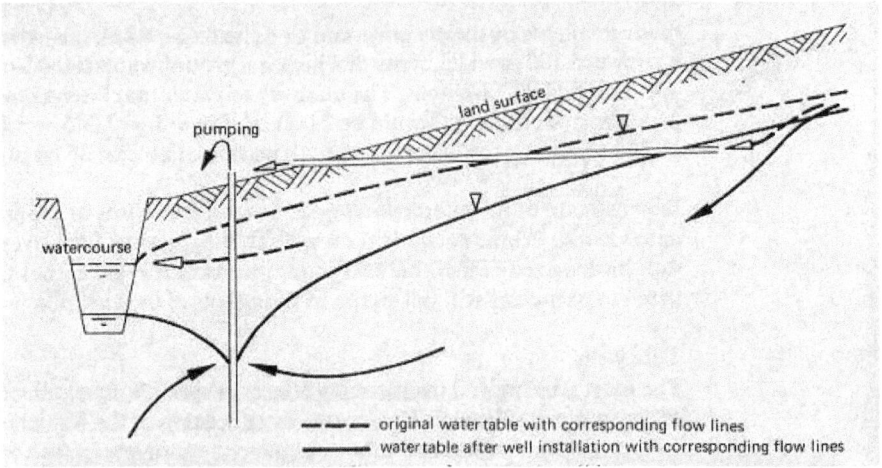

Illustration 99

Response:

_____

_____

_____

10. Without the Mesopotamians, buildings like this wouldn't exist. Why?

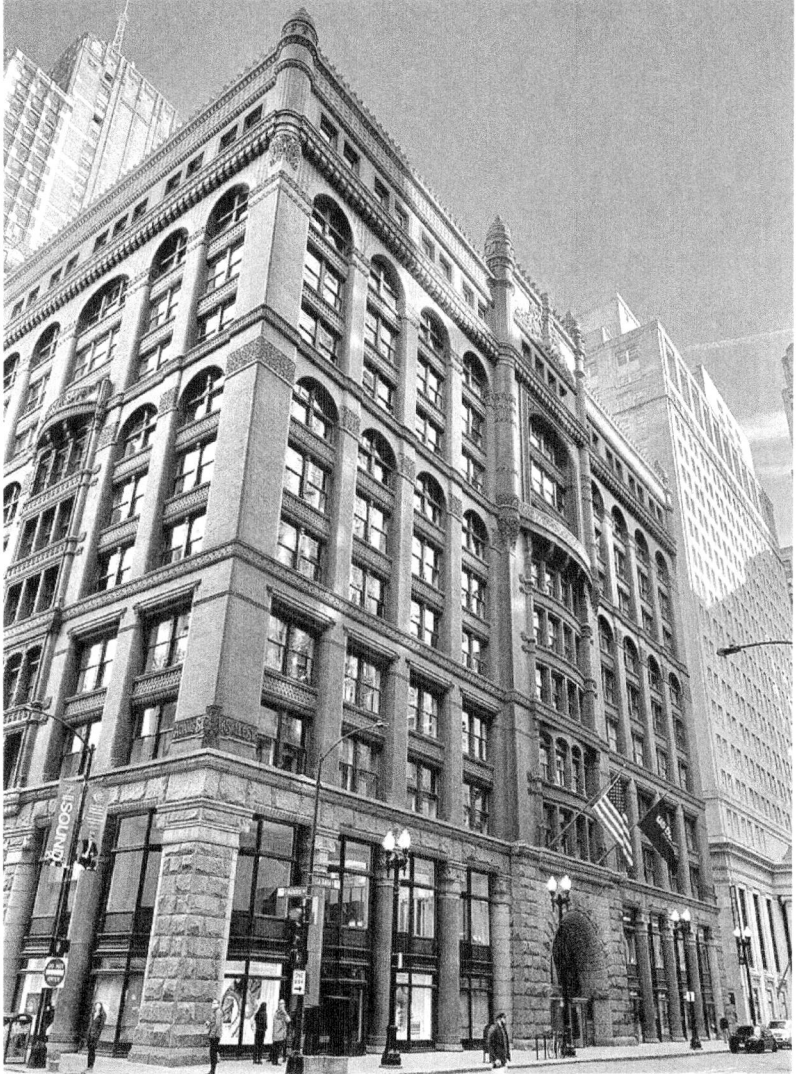

Illustration 100

Response:

_____

_____

_____

_____

Short Answer

1. How has Mesopotamian mythology influenced modern literature and media?

_____

_____

_____

2. How has Mesopotamian trade influenced the modern economy?

_____

_____

_____

3. What role did the Mesopotamian concept of governance play in developing a stable society?

_____

_____

_____

4. How did Mesopotamian technology impact modern technology?

_____

_____

_____

5. Mesopotamians made important contributions to medicine. How?

_____

_____

_____

6. What lessons can the Mesopotamians' ability to adapt to their environment teach modern societies?

_____

_____

_____

7. How has Mesopotamia influenced modern education?

_____

_____

_____

8. Discuss the effect of the Mesopotamian technological advances on modern living.

_____

_____

_____

9. When Mesopotamians settled beside the rivers, they had to learn much more than to grow their food. What else do you think they had to learn?

_____

_____

_____

10. How did the Mesopotamians teach the world how to keep records?

_____

_____

_____

Conclusion

Mesopotamia is the place where it all began. In the valley between two rivers, the foundation of modern civilization was laid. Hunter-gatherers have settled down, sowed crops, and brought the water to the dry land.

This dry land became the cradle of civilizations built on agriculture, innovation, and imagination. As their communities grew, so did their thriving farms and later sites. Producing more than they could use from some things and having no other essential resources, they thought, "Why not start trading what we have for what we need?"

This is how trading and later writing were invented. With so many deals to keep track of, the old-fashioned pictures didn't cut it anymore. So, cuneiform came, the revolutionary writing form that was useful for much more than trading.

Unfortunately, trading also led to the first conflicts and later wars in Mesopotamia – everyone wanted access to the best trading routes. The settlements and the city-states of the first official civilization couldn't always get along, and having different rules and trading methods did not help either.

Sargon, the founder of the first dynasty of the world, changed everything. Leading every former city-state he could conquer under his birth city's name (Akkadians), he built an empire like never before. Continuing in his footsteps, his successors maintained order the same way.

Other kings had slightly different approaches but similar results. They built a stronger and larger empire until they were defeated. Nevertheless, each of these empires amassed riches, knowledge, and skills that helped Mesopotamian civilization grow and leave a lasting legacy.

Amid conflicts and conquests, Mesopotamians arrived at transformative inventions, like the wheel, composite bow, metal helmets, powerful axes, and unique military tactics. Along with writing, these inventions have also transpired into contemporary uses.

Daily life in ancient Mesopotamia was anything but boring, although it often depended on a person's social status. Not everyone could afford to have leisurely time or get an education. However, those who were educated created a massive number of records that helped discover the nuanced cultural, religious, and ideological diversity that ruled the region.

Laws were established, changed, and established again until they finally resembled the ones used in modern legal systems. The monetary system also has roots in ancient Mesopotamian practices. From barter to token systems to the first coin, trade went through many phases, but finally, the concept of money was born, and it was here to stay.

The same can be said for scientific discoveries, medicine, or mathematics. From the 60-based system to the concept of zero, modern people have a lot to thank the Mesopotamians for.

Reading this book, you've learned about all these milestones and events, building a treasure trove of information about the colorful Mesopotamian civilization. You've also seen how they influenced modern societies, culture, art, and more.

Thank you for finishing this book, and congratulations on all the curious information you've learned. Hopefully, you had tons of fun with the trivia questions. If you do, don't forget to share your joy with others.

Answer Key

Chapter 1

Multiple Choice Questions

1. B. The territory of Mesopotamia is located between the Tigris and Euphrates rivers. These rivers travel from north to south, ending at the Persian Gulf. Most of the land is now known as the country of Iraq.

2. A and B. The Akkadian language is related to modern-day Hebrew and Arabic languages. All three languages belong to the Semitic language family – named after Shem, a son of Noah and the ancestor of all Arab and Jewish people.

3. B. The Code of Hammurabi was written on clay tablets and stone slabs. This form of writing was the most popular around 1754 B.C.E. when Hammurabi wrote this code.

4. C. The Code of Hammurabi determined punishment for crimes based on social status. For example, if a noble person hurt another noble person, they would have to be hurt the same way (i.e., if they broke the other person's arm, their arm would be broken too). Whereas if a noble person hurt a slave, they would only have to pay a fine.

5. D. The Code of Hammurabi was an early form of constitutional government because it gave people the chance to present evidence in their case, and everyone was seen as innocent until their guilt was proven. The adjustments based on social status

further added to the status of the early form of constitutional government.

6. A. The main social classes in ancient Mesopotamia were the kings, priests and nobility, lower classes, and slaves. The lower class included farmers, soldiers, and builders. There were also several classes of kings. Some ruled entire empires, while others only governed city-states.

7. A. After 2004 B.C.E., the Sumerian slowly disappeared as a spoken language. It was replaced by Akkadian. From then on, Sumerian was only used in religious ceremonies or to record tales and history.

8. A. and B. Sargon of Akkad was the ruler who transformed Sumer, the small city-state, into the world's first empire – the Akkadian Empire. According to his own autobiography, Sargon was abandoned by his mother as a baby but was chosen by the gods to rule and become the mighty king. However, some argue that Sargon only claimed this about himself to ensure he would be seen as a worthy ruler (After all, who could've been more worthy than some chosen by the gods?).

9. D. The Akkadians' most powerful enemies were the citizens of the city-state of Ebla. They also learned cuneiform writing and language but worshiped different gods. Some of their gods were the rivals of the Akkadian deities.

10. B. The Sumerian civilization had the strongest influence on the Elamites, the people living in southeast Mesopotamia (modern-day Iran). The center of this civilization was the city of Susa, where art and architecture were very similar to Sumerian.

True or False

1. True. The first code of laws, known as the Code of Ur-Nammu, was created in ancient Mesopotamia. It was carved on tablets by the Sumerians.

2. True. Due to the location of their settlements (between two large rivers), the early Mesopotamian civilization became specialized in agriculture. The more people started working in agriculture, the more they started to live close together – which is the definition of urban communities.

3. True. The early Mesopotamian civilization was formed from a mixture of Egyptian and Indus Valley civilizations. These brought together different cultures, languages, and religions and created a new civilization that had a huge impact on the history and growth of future civilizations.

4. False. Cuneiform writing was used for about 2000 years after it first appeared on archaic tablets. It was replaced in the first millennia when Phoenician writing was invented and put to use.

5. False. The Sumerians used excellent shipbuilding skills to travel overseas and reach other early civilizations on water.

6. False. The world's first dynastic empire was the Akkadian. It was founded by Sargon of Akkad in 2334 B.C.E.

7. True. The Assyrian empire was named after Ashur (also known as Ašur), the ancient city at the heart of the empire in northern Mesopotamia.

8. False. The Assyrian empire was much larger than its Akkadian ancestor, extending from the borders of Persia in the east to the borders of Egypt and Cyprus in the west.

9. True. Babylon was a small city from when it was established in 1894 B.C.E. until after 1792 B.C.E. when Hammurabi came to the throne. Under his rule, the city became the center of the famous Babylonian empire.

10. False. The Babylonian Empire was finally destroyed by the Macedonian king, Alexander the Great, in 335 around B.C.E.

Fill-in-the-Blank

1. The term Mesopotamian means the land between the rivers.

2. The world's oldest known city, Eridu, was located in ancient Mesopotamia.

3. One of the most important Mesopotamian inventions was writing.

4. Besides legal codes and writing, the Mesopotamians were also known for their use of technology.

5. Religion played an important role in Mesopotamian culture and life.

6. One of the world's first most famous stories, The Epic of Gilgamesh, was written in cuneiform.

7. Mesopotamians used cuneiform writing to write down <u>legends</u> and <u>letters</u> to one another and record <u>important dates</u> and <u>sales</u>.

8. The Sumerians were excellent <u>ship</u>-builders, creating vessels to · travel across the <u>Persian Gulf</u>.

9. Sumerian religion was <u>polytheistic</u>, and their gods often had <u>human</u> form.

10. In Sumer, the centers of the cities were the temples built on enormous ziggurats.

Myth Buster: Common Misconceptions about Mesopotamia

The Hanging Gardens of Babylon

The Hanging Gardens of Babylon didn't exist – or at least not in the way they were, as described in Mesopotamian mythology. According to this, in Babylon, there were gardens built on terraces several stories up in the air. There were several layers of garden terraces, which thrived with the most beautiful flowers and greenery.

The only problem was that Babylon was in the middle of a desert-like area, where water was hard to come by. According to historians, watering the hanging gardens would be an impossible task. Moreover, no archeological excavation was ever able to discover any traces of this mythical garden.

Not All Gods Control Nature

In popular culture, Mesopotamian gods and goddesses are often pictured as fierce entities who can summon the powers of nature in an instant. In reality, some Mesopotamian gods and goddesses also helped people and their communities learn new skills, defeat their rivals, and survive tough times.

Some deities aided the work of scribes (writers), while others guided metalworkers in creating the best weapons. Others helped those wanting to learn the ancient art of traditional medicine. Some gods and goddesses guarded specific cities and communities.

While some Mesopotamian deities were working together with nature, their number was far fewer than the number of gods and goddesses who helped people.

Picture-Based Questions

1. Cuneiform writing. The carved wedges made it easy for the Sumerians to record whatever they wanted. For example, this

clay tablet holds the records of the amount of silver prepared food a governor. It dates to around 2500 B.C.E.

2. This is a votive wall plaque that was likely used in religious buildings or ceremonies.

3. The Ziggurat of Ur has a stepped tower built of mud-brick with a flat top. At its summit stood a roofed structure that housed the sacred idol or image of the temple's deity. The temple complex also included the homes of the priests, workshops for artisans who made goods for the temple, and storage facilities to meet the needs of the temple workers.

4. The Akkadian Empire – the world's first true empire. This was the territory of the empire around 2200 B.C.E., under its first ruler, Sargon of Akkad.

5. Alexander the Great, the king of Macedonia, conquered the Persian Empire in the 4th century.

6. The Empire of Ur. It was led by Ur-Namma, who recorded the law code of Ur-Nammu.

7. All the neighboring and rival empires near the Babylonian Empire, including the Hittites, would soon attack Babylon. (The direction of the oncoming attack is shown with the arrow.)

8. These are helmets from the Assyrian Empire.

9. Sargon II greatly admired his namesake, Sargon the Great. He wanted to establish just as strong of a realm as Sargon did when he founded the world's first multicultural empire.

10. The city of Nineveh - a great city from the Assyrian period. With 15 gateways, the city was just as impressive as Babylon.

A Day in the Life of a Sumerian Teen

Sumerian teens began their days by going to school. Education was very important in middle and upper social classes, so children were expected to pay attention in school and learn their lessons. One of their main subjects was writing, which they had to practice on clay tablets. Children were supervised by teachers, and if they didn't learn their lessons or didn't pay attention, they were punished.

Back home, Sumerian teens were expected to practice their schoolwork even more. They also had chores to do at home. If the family had animals, the teens had to help take care of them. Girls were given more chores in the house (for example, they had to help prepare lunch and dinner and clean up). Boys were given tasks around the home, or sometimes they went hunting with their fathers.

In their free time, Sumerian teens liked doing sports like wrestling or swimming. At night, the family would gather together. The older members would tell stories, and the children would listen in awe. If the family had a talented singer or musician, they would perform. Some teens would play the flute or harp.

The next day, they would begin their day again by putting on sandals and clothes made of animal skin and head to school.

Timeline Questions

1. Sumerian

   Akkadian

   Assyrian

   Babylonian

2. Earliest civilizations formed in Mesopotamia – according to archaeological records, the earliest civilizations in Mesopotamia were formed around 12000 B.C.E.

   Agriculture became common – The Mesopotamians had a thriving agriculture by 6000 B.C.E.

   The first larger civilization appears – The first of the largest Mesopotamian civilizations, the Sumerian, appeared between 4000 and 6000 B.C.E.

   First recorded writing – The first recorded writing in human history appeared around 3000 B.C.E. in the Sumerian civilization.

3. The oldest wheel – The oldest wheel in the world dates back to 3500 B.C.E. and is the height of the Sumerian civilization.

   The cultural interchange with the Akkadians begins – The Sumerians began a large cultural interchange with their northern neighbors, the Akkadians, around 3000 B.C.E.

   Sumerians are under the rule of the Akkadian Empire – By 2334 B.C.E., the Sumerians were under the rule of the Akkadians.

   The approximate date of the writing of the Epic of Gilgamesh. – While the exact date of this famous Sumerian (and possibly the first written story in history) cannot be determined, historians place its creation to around 2100-1200 B.C.E.

4. The collapse of the Akkadian Empire - After 180 years of existence, the Akkadian Empire collapsed in 2154 B.C.E.

   The rule of the Assyrian Empire - After the collapse of the Akkadian Empire, the control of major parts of Mesopotamia was seized by the Assyrians. They held it for the next 1400 years (until the 7th century B.C.E.).

   Babylon is founded - Babylon, the city that became the center of a later Mesopotamian empire, was founded in 1894 B.C.E.

   Babylonians conquered southern Mesopotamia - The Babylonian civilization took control of southern Mesopotamia under the rule of Hammurabi from 1792 to 1750 B.C.E.

5. Code of Hammurabi was written around 1754 B.C.E. when the 6th Babylonian king Hammurabi ordered the writing of a new code of laws called the Code of Hammurabi. It was a collection of old and improved codes of law from the previous Mesopotamian empires.

   The first invasion of Babylon - Babylon was a great power in the region until it was invaded and destroyed in 1531 B.C.E.

   The Rise of the Neo-Babylonian Empire - After its destruction, the Babylonian civilization was reformed and became just as powerful as the Neo-Babylonian Empire between 626 B.C.E. and 539 B.C.E.

   Persians conquered Babylon - the Neo-Babylonian Empire was conquered by the Persians in 539 B.C.E.

6. The rise of agriculture came first, but the ancient Mesopotamians lived in small communities for two millennia afterward. Their cities began to grow only after 5500 B.C.E.

7. The Sumerians wrote on clay tablets first and later baked the tablets. Baking made the tablets more durable (similar to how Mesopotamian building bricks were made), and the writing could be preserved for a long time.

8. The fall of the Akkadian Empire in 2193 B.C.E. led to many protests and uprisings, including the rising of the Gutian people. These northern barbarians wanted to take control of the empire.

   The king of the city of Ur and the ruler of Ur-Namma took control over the former Akkadian territories after 2100 B.C.E.

   Ur-Namma was attacked by the Amorites and Elamites in 2004

B.C.E. The Amorites finally took control and founded Babylonia.

9. The Hittites, the civilization living in Syria and Anatolia, conquered the Babylonians around 1595 B.C.E.

The Assyrian Empire's role was to control the place inhabited by the Hittites around 1365 B.C.E.

The Assyrians conquered Israel around the beginning of the 8th century B.C.E.

The new Assyrian dynasty was divided into provinces by Sargon II in 722 B.C.E.

10. Alexander the Great invaded the Persian Empire in 331 B.C.E. By this time, most of the ancient Mesopotamian cities had already been destroyed, and the culture had been overtaken by the previous conquerors.

Chapter 2

Multiple Choice

1. B. Anu, one of the three main Mesopotamian gods, was the king of the gods and the god of the sky. The Sumerian word "An" means "heaven," indicating the deities' reign. Over time, Anu became more powerful, ruling over the entire pantheon by the time of the Babylonian Empire.

2. D. Anu, Enlil, and Ea ruled over all the spirits, lower gods, and the entire universe. In the later stories, they give control to Marduk, the son of Ea.

3. A. Sumerian is a language that becomes cuneiform in written form. The Sumerian isn't a religion or cult because Sumerians did not have their own unique religion. They adopted many of their beliefs from the other nations.

4. B. Ninib, Shamash, and Nergal are the three solar deities of the Mesopotamian pantheon (they rule over the sun and its effects on people's environment).

5. C. Ea and Nebo are the main water deities in Mesopotamia.

6. B. and D. The different regions had different ways to worship certain gods. These gods were associated with the region. For example, in Eridu, Ea was worshiped through rituals that were only performed in this area.

7. D. The concept of the "Seven gods who decree" was developed by historians studying the Assyrian pantheon. The seven gods were all given powers, ruling over everything else. Many argue that this can't be applied because some regions had different deities, and the seven gods were not one of them.

8. A. Enuma Elish is often seen as a central text to Mesopotamian mythology, though it doesn't include all gods and goddesses. Therefore, it can be used to understand the entire Mesopotamian pantheon and its influence.

9. D. Historians can trace the origin of all Mesopotamian deities for several reasons. The same gods had different roles in different areas, appearing several times in the genealogy tree. Others had no clear origins, while some were only vaguely mentioned as spouses of a deity, but it wasn't clear where they came from.

10. C. In all stories, Nanna and Ningal are Inanna's parents. In different stories, they had other children, too, but their names varied from region to region and era to era during Mesopotamian history.

True or False

1. True. The Epic of Gilgamesh is one of the earliest known works of literary fiction. However, historians suggest that many more similar stories could've been written before this piece but haven't survived to the modern age.

2. True. In the story *Inanna and the God of Wisdom*, Ea is the wisdom who gives Inanna the meh (the divine essence that she gives to humanity). Ea is usually shown as a friendly and caring god who always wants to help people.

3. False. Mesopotamians believed that people were created to serve the gods. For the same reason, they built temples for the deities, offered food and sacrifice to them, and wrote songs and stories about their divine powers.

4. False. Stories of destruction by gods are common in Mesopotamian history because the Mesopotamians believed that they could never serve their deities well enough. One mistake could be enough to anger a god or goddess, and they would destroy everything in their way.

5. True. The Mesopotamians believed that the gods would punish them even in the afterlife, which was called "the land of no return." It was described as a dark and unfriendly place where the gods punish people by letting them become consumed by guilt over all the mistakes they made and the people who left behind.

6. False. In the early days, the Sumerians had no concept of god. Only after they started interacting with the Semites did they start to develop the idea of a god. Until then, they believed that everything in the world has a spirit or essence.

7. True. Mesopotamian gods and goddesses rule over things and events people interact with every day. For example, they created gods for water, storms, the sun, the moon, enemies, etc.

8. False. The Mesopotamian deities did not appear often. They could be kind, but they could only be worshiped from afar.

9. True. The political and societal events shaped the makeup of the Mesopotamian pantheon. When Sumerians started developing the concept of god, there were only a handful of deities. By the time the Babylonian Empire started rising in power, the number of deities increased to over 3,000.

10. True. With so many gods and goddesses in their pantheon, the Babylonians started ranking their major deities in a hierarchical numerical order at the beginning of the second millennium B.C. E.

Epic Tales: Stories from Ancient Mesopotamia

The *Epic of Gilgamesh* is probably the most famous story in the world – given its age and heroes (all of whom were important characters in Mesopotamian mythology). The epic recounts the story of Gilgamesh, the son of the king of Uruk, as he journeys through the land and encounters many difficulties and triumphs. These include defeating his overlord Akka and the Bull of Heaven sent by the goddess Inanna after Gilgamesh refused her love. The hero was accompanied by his faithful sidekick Enkidu and his own strength, of which he is unaware. During his journey, he learns his own strengths and weaknesses and finds peace, even after he learns that he will not be granted immortality like some other heroes were.

Inanna's Descent is the story of the rescue of the goddess Inanna from the underworld. Inanna goes to the underworld to visit her sister,

Ereshkigal, the queen of the underworld. Ereshkigal isn't happy to see her, strips her of her clothes and other possessions, and later kills her. Enki, Inanna's father, sends two creatures to rescue her, and she is revived with the food and water of life. This story talks about rebirth but also about the importance of letting go of a person's possessions. It may be scary, but it sets you free, and once you're free, you can become a new version of yourself.

Fill-in-the-Blank

1. The Mesopotamian goddess of love and war is named Ishtar.

2. The Babylonian god of death and illness is called Irra.

3. The Sumerians also had another goddess of love. Her name is Inanna.

4. Abgal is one of the seven sages often depicted carrying a bucket and a cone of incense for purification.

5. The Mesopotamian god of sweet and fresh water is Absu. He was killed by his son Ea.

6. The Babylonians offered their gratitude to Arazu when the building was completed.

7. The Sumerian "Mistress of Animals," Baba, was a local mother goddess.

8. The Babylonian god of grain and fertility, Dagon, was worshiped near the midsection of the Euphrates.

9. As the mother of the hero-turned-god Marduk, Damkina also had a major role in the Babylonian pantheon.

10. The Babylonian god of wisdom is named Ea or Enki.

Picture Based Questions

1. This Ea, the water god – Is depicted with the cup he uses to let water flow. In the Sumerian Empire, Ea was known as Enki.

2. It is a male worshiper who has likely participated in religious ceremonies. Besides priests, other worshippers were also given important roles and became respected members of the community based on their ability to help out in religious rituals.

3. This is Anzu, the fire-breathing creature who appears in many tales from the Sumerian, Akkadian, and Babylonian empires. In one, the tale of The Huluppu Tree, Anzu infests the tree of Inanna. In another story, he steals the Tablets of Destiny after he

is charged with watching them.

4. Ashur is the Assyrian supreme god, and a local deity connected to the city of Assur. In Assyrian mythology, he is also known as The Lord of the Whole Heavens, and his name means "whole heaven."

5. The serpent/fish god is Basmu, ruler of birth. He also works together with birth goddesses in some of his tales.

6. The Bull of Heaven, or Gugalanna, was associated with the Queen of the Underworld, Ereshkigal. However, its master was Anu, the sky god.

7. The marriage of Dumuzi and Inanna. Dumuzi is the patron of shepherds and fertility. When Inanna is killed and sent to the underworld, Dumuzi takes her place and remains in the underworld instead.

8. The Sumerian god of the air, Enlil, was also known as the Lord of the Air and Wind and the Holder of The Tablets of Destiny. According to some records, Enlil was the ruler of the Sumerian pantheon.

9. This is the goddess Gula, or Bau. She was often depicted as a dog and was the patron of healing and doctors.

10. The Babylonian King of the Gods, Marduk, was not only a deity but a great hero. He defeated Tiamat and his forces of chaos.

Match the God to the Domain

1. Anu —Sky.
2. Ereshkigal – Underworld.
3. Geshtianna – Fertility.
4. Damu – Healing.
5. Zababa – War.
6. Nusku – Fire.
7. Nergal – Death.
8. Haya —Grain.
9. Asalluhi – Magic.
10. Papsukkal – Gate-keeping.

Chapter 3

1. C. Both the Tigris and the Euphrates were known for unpredictable flooding, which was crucial for improving Mesopotamian agriculture.

2. D. In and near the rivers, the Mesopotamians found reed for construction, fish for food, water for irrigation, drinking, and more.

3. B. The marshes provide connections to the Persian trading route. They connected to the Tigris and Euphrates, which end in the Persian Gulf, opening up opportunities for long-distance travel.

4. A. and B. Upper Mesopotamians had access to mountains and forests, where they could firewood and hunt animals for food, clothes, and shelter. They also had access to land routes to areas where they could obtain resources like obsidian, a type of rock they often used to make cutting tools.

5. A. The Agricultural Revolution led to the Urban Revolution. The more people saw the benefits of farming near the rivers, the more they moved to the settlements on the wetlands. New settlements were also established near the Tigris and the Euphrates.

6. A. The retreating wetlands left the settlements with areas that required more irrigation. The farmers were forced to work harder and coordinate their efforts to obtain the necessary water for their crops.

7. C. The irregular floodings oversaturated the land with water. As a result, the water couldn't drain toward the sea and remained logged in the soil. It needed to be drained away so crops could be cultivated.

8. D. Mesopotamia has many wetlands forms near the Tigris and the Euphrates. These include deltas, estuaries, and marshes.

9. B. The Tigris and the Euphrates were surrounded by both permanent and seasonal marshes.

10. B. and C. The Mesopotamian wetlands were used as a water resource to substitute for rainfall. They made growing healthy crops without irrigation easier.

The Twin Lifelines: Tigris and Euphrates

Tigris and Euphrates are the two rivers infusing water and life into what became known as the Mesopotamian region. They're two twins trickling from the area now belonging to western Syria and down to the Persian Gulf. Between them lies a valley where civilizations were born.

In itself, the valley and the vast area around the rivers are very dry (like most of the Middle East). However, the Tigris and the Euphrates aren't just regular rivers. They Are temperamental, often flooding the areas between and around them.

Noticing that the flooded areas could be used for farming and agriculture, the first settlers decided to try their luck and use the properties of the area to their advantage. They succeed – thanks to some master planning and organizational skills.

Fortunately, they had the rivers for irrigation and the surrounding mountains and forests for wood, shelter, and food resources to help out. Soon, the small settlements around the fertile wetlands near the twin rivers grew and became urban cities where most people earn a living from agriculture.

True or False

1. True. Due to the extensive and unpredictable floodings, the Mesopotamians were forced to build canal systems to direct the water to the lands and ensure proper irrigation.

2. True. Besides the unpredictable flooding, the Mesopotamian climate also became drier. This meant fewer natural marches and more drier areas that needed to be irrigated.

3. False. Mesopotamian civilization did not develop in the same way throughout the entire region. Urban societies developed mainly in the Lower and Upper Mesopotamian areas, whereas the other regions were scarcely populated.

4. True. One of the main reasons Mesopotamia became the cradle of civilization about 7-6,000 years ago is because it lay in a wetter area. It didn't happen anywhere else in the Middle East because everything was drier, and agriculture couldn't thrive anywhere else.

5. False. The two rivers were very unpredictable, which meant they sometimes caused more harm than good. For example, the Nile in Egypt flooded approximately the same time every year, which

put the Egyptian neighbors in a better position throughout the year.

6. True. The earliest cities of southern Mesopotamia were founded on the edges of a great marsh that provided plenty of natural resources for food and construction.

7. False. According to historians, in Upper Mesopotamia, the rainfall was reliable enough that irrigation was rarely necessary. In Lower Mesopotamia, the rainfall was less predictable, and irrigation was needed most of the time.

8. False. The small Sumerian settlements around the river evolved into cities roughly around 3000 - 2500 B.C.E.

9. False. Despite the regular floodings, Mesopotamia was not suitable for living and farming even before the marshes retreated. There was very little rain, which made growing crops almost impossible without irrigation.

10. True. Northern Mesopotamian was mountainous and less suitable for agriculture. It grew much slower, and the south overtook it around 4000 B.C.E.

Fill-in-the-Blank

1. The Atrahasis is an ancient Mesopotamian story that includes a great flood similar to the biblical tale of Noah's Ark.

2. The vicinity of the rivers and wetlands made it easier to organize small-scale local irrigation and eliminated the need for transporting water from farther away.

3. In the beginning, Mesopotamian farmers mainly cultivated wheat and barley. Later on, they established gardens where they could also grow beans, peas, lentils, cucumbers, leeks, lettuce, garlic, grapes, apples, melons, and figs.

4. As the Agricultural Revolution continued, the Mesopotamians also began to keep cows, sheep, goats, and cows for their milk and meat.

5. Each year, the floods of the twin rivers brought silt to the land – leaving the farmers with a mixture of rich, humid soil and tiny rocks.

6. In the valleys between the Tigris and the Euphrates, the intense sun made living and farming even harder without irrigation.

7. Early Mesopotamians learned to adapt to their <u>environments</u>, especially to available <u>water resources</u> that served their <u>community</u>.

8. The first civilization went without rain for <u>eight</u> months of the year.

9. The development of irrigation also led to a quick <u>economic</u> development.

10. To ensure the water levels were always balanced in all lands, Mesopotamian farmers often <u>scooped water</u> from one water tank into another.

Floods and Fables: River Tales in Mesopotamia

Besides the source of water and fish, the twin rivers were also fertile grounds for many myths circulating through the Mesopotamian culture. These included stories about the flooding (similar to the Great Flood story), the deities governing the rivers and their movement, and more.

According to one fable, Enki (Ea), the water god, warned people about another god causing a flood, prompting a human hero to save the day. According to another story, Enki wanted to protect the rivers and told people they shouldn't make noise around the water. A third story talks about Enki giving water and fish to the rivers so they could feed people.

Religious ceremonies asking gods and goddesses for help, cultural events like celebrations, and even burials took place at the twin rivers. Some cities had local deities who guarded the waters and the lives of the people the waters sustained.

Picture Based Questions

1. You'll notice Babylon appearing in the lower part of the map. The Euphrates is the river flowing next and upwards from it. On the other side of the Euphrates is Tigris.

2. The area is called Fertile Crescent for two reasons. It was one of the places where the Agricultural Revolution could thrive without too many limitations. More importantly, the area was fertile because many inventions and innovations originated from it.

3. Gilgamesh conquered many beasts (he is shown defeating a lion) and became the oldest-known hero in literary fiction. According to the legends, to protect his grave, the Euphrates was diverted, the grave was dug up, and after the burial, the river was returned

to its bank.

4. They're called marshes or wetlands. They were created by frequent floodings, heavy rainfalls, and the accumulation of snow melting from the nearby Persian and Turkish mountains.

5. According to Mesopotamian mythology, Ea (or Enki) gave water to the rivers. The picture shows the god with water flowing from his shoulders and into the river bank.

6. The rivers were also used to transport a lot of goods, which enabled trading with other nations.

7. This is Lake Hazer, located near Elazig, Turkey.

8. The picture shows that the two rivers are not only working together to nurture the Mesopotamian region but also join into one large river. After joining, they quickly empty into the Persian Gulf.

9. This was the ancient Sumerian city of Shuruppak, from where some of the earliest Sumerian literary works came from.

10. The connections to the Indus Valley Civilizations (another important empire at the time) were made possible by water trading through the Tigris and Euphrates rivers and the Persian Gulf.

Short Answer

1. The Tigris and the Euphrates rivers provided the perfect environment for the Agricultural Revolution in Mesopotamia. They offered a precious resource, water, in the otherwise dry climate where agriculture wouldn't have been possible.

2. The countries that now lie where Mesopotamia once was are Iraq, Kuwait, Turkey, and Syria.

3. One of the first Mesopotamian cities to reach a population of 50,000 (all thriving on agriculture) was Uruk.

4. Many of the innovations were a result of an attempt to make agriculture more efficient (for example, some were related to the organization of irrigation or harvest).

5. In Upper (northern) Mesopotamia, people remained in small settlements, living in close but tiny communities and relying on each other to help out with irrigation and farming.

6. The levels of water in the Tigris and Euphrates rivers depended on the amount of rainfall in the east.

7. The flooding was very damaging, often covering the entire farmland, killing animals, and washing away people's homes.

8. They led away excess water during the flooding and protected people's houses and property.

9. They built banks on the banks of Tigris and Euphrates. The banks held back the water when the rivers threatened to overflow.

10. With efficient agriculture and water resource use, fewer people were needed in the industry, and more people could do something else, like learning new skills and inventing something new – both of which helped the civilization grow and advance.

Chapter 4

Multiple Choice Questions

1. B. In the early days, cuneiform was written on clay tablets. These made creating and preserving the text much easier, making them perfect for record keeping.

2. C. When cuneiform became a phonetic script, each letter (symbol) meant a syllable. They were carved based on the sounds of their syllables. This way, the Sumerians could record everything in their language without anything being lost in translation.

3. D. Merchants used cuneiform to record their sales and contracts. Employers used it to write down the salary they paid to their workers. Recordkeepers used it to record taxes, contributions, and other money due to the rulers. Priests used to record religious texts and other important events.

4. B. The earliest form of cuneiform used by traders and temple officials to record the movement of goods were pictures of items. These are known as pictographs.

5. B. The scribes carved the wedge-shaped symbols into clay tablets with a reed stylus cut.

6. B. Cuneiform writing was in use for over 3000 years across the world. During this time, it was adopted into 15 different languages. Besides Sumerian, Akkadian, Assyrian, and Babylonian, these included Elamite, Old Persian, Hittite,

Urartian, and Hungarian, among others.

7. D. Assyrian. Most of what historians learned about ancient Mesopotamia comes from Assyrian records (many of which were written in cuneiform).

8. C. Venus. The observations of Venus were created during the reign of Babylonian king Ammisaduqa.

9. D. Being able to read and write alone separated scribes from the other members of their community. They had an important social status, and it took them years to gain the title of a scribe.

10. A. The building where scribes learned to read and write was called a Tablet House (or Edubba in Sumerian, which literally translates as "House of Tablets"). It was an early form of school where Mesopotamian students went to receive and learn lessons.

Cuneiform: The World's First Writing System

Cuneiform, the world's first writing system, dates back to 3000 B.C.E. The earliest evidence of cuneiform use was the Sumerian temple records, where administrators wrote down amounts of stored goods.

The earliest writings were simple pictures of the items that needed to be recorded. Then, wedge-shaped signs were put together to represent sounds. Now, the writing could represent the Sumerian language.

To further simplify the representations on the tablets, strokes began to convey concepts by association instead of the meaning of the words that describe the concepts. For example, instead of describing someone as honorable, they would just write honor.

Writing allowed the Mesopotamians to show many new concepts, which were hard to show with pictures and simple symbols. For example, they were now able to write about the fear of death (a common fear in the Mesopotamian culture), whereas before, they could only picture death and what they thought awaited them afterward.

True or False

1. False. Mesopotamians used cuneiform to record everything in their language – not just religious texts.

2. True. Many sacred texts from Mesopotamia were preserved on clay tablets – written in cuneiform and passed on through generations.

3. True. Rulers used cuneiform and not just to keep up with their tasks and dues. They also wrote laws governing communities or the entire empire.

4. True. To form the wedge shapes with specific meanings, cuneiform writing required a steady hand and precise movements.

5. True. While it's not entirely clear where cuneiform originates from, some historians suggest that it could be the next step in the evolution of earlier accounting techniques.

6. True. The marks were not only precise but also looked the same every time, making it easier to recognize and learn them.

7. False. The Epic of Gilgamesh was translated into several other languages early on. This was proven by the discovery of tablets with the story in non-Sumerian cuneiform. Some of these were found in Hattusas (in the Hittites), Emar (Syria), and Megiddo (Levant).

8. False. Clay tablets with maps of Mesopotamia were found – along with cuneiform writing indicating places and directions on the map. The center of this world map (as they were called) was Babylon.

9. False. In the early days of Mesopotamian civilization, there were very few people who could write. Those who could be called scribes.

10. False. Most scribes were men because men had more rights to education (or in life in general). Women had to follow different rules, and learning was rarely one of them.

Fill-in-the-Blank

1. The famous Mesopotamian ruler, King Hammurabi, created one of the earliest law codes written in cuneiform.

2. The term "cuneiform" originates from the Latin cuneus word, which means "wedge."

3. Writing gives meaning to a symbol, similar to how Mesopotamian priests interpreted divine signs for looking into the future.

4. Cuneiform was a very complex writing system, and some texts could only be written and interpreted by scribes.

5. Although created over 4000 years ago, cuneiform writing was only deciphered in the <u>19th century C.E.</u>

6. Cuneiform writing first appeared in Sumerian cities with <u>centralized</u> economies.

7. Temple officials used cuneiform to record the amount of <u>grain</u> and the number of <u>animals</u> leaving or entering their storages.

8. Besides simple recordings like lists, there were also <u>letters</u> enclosed in <u>clay</u> envelopes.

9. Assyrian kings had <u>libraries</u> full of records in <u>cuneiform</u> script.

10. The longest cuneiform literary work is the <u>Epic of Gilgamesh</u>.

Picture Based Questions

1. This tablet contains a hymn to Marduk, the Babylonian hero-god. It is dated around the 1st millennium B.C.E., at the height of the Babylonian Empire.

2. The map of Nippur around 1500 B.C.E.

3. The tablet was used to record important information. It was used as an "exercise sheet" for students. Scribes spent many hours practicing cuneiform symbols and used plenty of spare tablets like this. It's like how small children practice writing in spare notebooks in modern days.

4. This tablet shows a ritual scene, and it was once hung at the entrance of a temple in Uruk. The city of Uruk holds some of the most important evidence of how the Mesopotamians shifted from pictographs to phonograms.

5. She was the goddess Nisaba. Formerly, she was the goddess of agriculture, but when writing became popular, she was transformed into the patron goddess of writing and scribes. In some sources, she is also mentioned as the scribe of the gods.

6. This is a statue of a Sumerian scribe. It was dedicated to the god Ningirsu. It wasn't uncommon for scribes to dedicate statues of themselves and their profession to gods and goddesses. They believed that helped them learn, practice, and gain a higher social status.

7. The tablet contains a list of synonyms – something young scribes could use at the beginning of their career. The more words they were able to write, the better.

8. These are instructions for the Royal Game of Ur. This game is almost 5000 years old and still exists today. The rules were written by a Babylonian astronomer in 177 B.C.E., but the game was invented much before that, likely sometime in the early days of ancient Mesopotamia.

9. She was Enheduanna, the daughter of the famous ruler Sargon of Akkad. Enheduanna was given the opportunity to learn writing and later became a priestess and a poet. One of her most important works was the Hymns to Inanna.

10. The city of Nineveh, the capital of the Neo-Assyrian Empire. The tablets likely belonged to the collection of King Ashurbanipal, who ruled from 669 B.C.E. to 631 B.C.E.

From Clay to Papyrus: Writing Materials in Ancient Times

In the early days, Sumerians wrote only on clay tablets molded from wet clay found at the riverside. They used a reed or stick stylus to carve the symbols in the wet clay and left the tablet under the sun to dry.

The tablets varied in size, and the text varied in length. Sometimes, it would take up to 12 tablets if the text was particularly long.

Later on, Mesopotamian scribes also began to write on metal, ivory, and glass objects, as well as pottery. These objects usually contained more formal texts, like instructions for religious ceremonies or letters to kings. To write in these materials, the scribes needed harder and sharper tools made from ivory, bone, or iron.

Papyrus was invented in ancient Egypt around 3000 B.C.E., but it only made its way into Mesopotamia much later. When it became available, the Mesopotamians started using it as a writing surface – as it conveniently held much more information and was easier to store.

To write on papyrus, they had to use delicate brushes because any other writing tool would damage the delicate surface.

Short Answer

1. Cuneiform writing had many uses – all of which contributed to the growth of the society. Contracts became more reliable (and more people wanted to do them), cultural traditions were preserved, and laws were born.

2. As the number of people in the settlements grew, so did the number of transactions and goods trading places. Tracking where everything ventured became very difficult – until cuneiform

writing was introduced.

3. Simple marks were created first, and after them, the signs and symbols were adjusted to represent the sounds of a spoken language.

4. Each student was assigned an older student to help with the lessons. These older students were called big brothers, who also punished students who didn't learn their lessons.

5. Mathematics and writing in cuneiform general were the two most important subjects in Mesopotamian scribe schools. Students learned not only Sumerian cuneiform but also Akkadian.

6. Clay tablets with cuneiform writing are part of an ancient heritage. They Are remnants of a civilization that shaped the ones that came after and those that are yet to come.

7. The early version of cuneiform contains pictures with precise and direct meaning. They were used during long-distance trading, where showing what you're recording as quickly as possible was very important.

8. Cuneiform writing became more complex during the Early Dynastic Period, between 2900 B.C.E. and 2330 B.C.E.

9. More people wanted to learn how to write but didn't always have the means for education. Sometimes, they needed a little help, so they "borrowed" powers from a deity who otherwise had a different role.

10. Despite introducing new meanings and soundings, the number of cuneiform characters was reduced from 1.000 to 600.

Chapter 5

Multiple Choice Questions

1. B. The world's first empire in Mesopotamia, the Akkadian Empire, was created by Sargon of Akkad (also known as Sargon the Great). Ruling between 2334 and 2279 B.C.E., Sargon conquered many Sumerian settlements and united them under his rule.

2. A. Gilgamesh was the king of Uruk. As the fifth king of the city, he always showed courage – which perhaps inspired the tales about his heroic deeds. In some sources, he is described as a demigod with superhuman strength (but not a true deity).

3. C. The sixth king of the city-state Babylon was Hammurabi, who also founded the world-famous Babylonian Empire. He ruled from 1792 to 1752 B.C.E.

4. In the mid-7th century B.C.E., King Nabopolassar allied himself with the enemy Mendes' rule so he could gain assistance in conquering the magnificent (and well-protected) city of the city of Nineveh. The fall of the city of Nineveh also meant the end of the Assyrian Empire.

5. D. The first Assyrian Empire was founded by Shamshi-Adad I, who ruled from 1813 to 1791 B.C.E. He was a great leader who had excellent skills for organizing his army on the battlefield.

6. D. Darius I made quite an impression when he invaded Greece – although his army was eventually defeated by the Greeks.

7. B. When the Mesopotamian king couldn't handle both civil and religious duties, he began to share his responsibility and governing power with the high priest.

8. B. In ancient times, trade caused many wars, especially in Mesopotamia and its surroundings, where there were few resources, and everyone tried to secure the source of precious resources for themselves.

9. C. In the first Akkadian Empire, Sargon united 65 different city-states.

10. D. The downfall of the Akkadian government was caused by the Gutians. This was a surprise to the Akkadians, who, since Sargon's rule, believed that the gods were always in their favor.

True or False

1. True. The Code of Hammurabi isn't only one of the first law codes in the world, but it's also one of the longest documents ever translated from cuneiform.

2. False. While Sargon did much to strengthen the city-states under his rule, the empire he founded reached its peak under another king, Naram-Sin.

3. False. The Northern and South Mesopotamian Empires were united in 539 B.C.E. Until then, they existed separately, even though the North grew much slower – which eventually caused its downfall and assimilation to the South.

4. True. While Ashurbanipal amassed much wealth and power, the empire went into a sharp decline. The cultural heritage was lost, and the cities were slowly destroyed.

5. False. Cyrus the Great established the Persian Empire, but the empire did not reach its peak until the reign of Darius I.

6. True. In the First Persian War, the Persians lost a battle under the rule of Darius I. King Xerxes I returned to conquer Greece but was also defeated and forced to quickly return to Persia.

7. True. During his rule between 580 and 530 B.C.E., the first king of the Persian Empire, Cyrus the Great, allowed the Jews to return to their Jerusalem homes.

8. True. Kingship in Mesopotamia existed at least since the Uruk period (around 3600 B.C.E.). By contrast, the first empire was founded over a millennia later, around 26300 B.C.E.

9. False. Before the Akkadian Empire was funded, the city-states had rulers but were not under the direct control of one unified administration like a king.

10. False. The city-states united under the Akkadian Empire were not satisfied with the government. It wasn't because they objected to the rules but because they were treated like occupied territory. Their new rulers were not concerned about any of their needs but expected them to accept anything they ordered.

Fill-in-the-Blank

1. The Assyrian Empire was known for its powerful army and excellent <u>warfare</u> skills.

2. Ruling from 2254 to 2218 B.C.E., Naram-Sin was Sargon's <u>grandson</u> and the first Mesopotamian ruler, claiming to be a <u>deity</u>.

3. After conquering them, Nebuchadnezzar II sent the <u>Jews</u> into exile.

4. King Sennacherib conquered <u>Babylon</u> and rebuilt the city of <u>Nineveh</u>, turning it into one of the most stunning cities in ancient history.

5. The last truly powerful king of the Assyrian Empire was <u>Ashurbanipal</u>.

6. Sargon the Great claimed that his military success was due to guidance he received from the goddess <u>Inanna</u>.

7. One of the lesser-known inventions originating from Mesopotamia is the concept of <u>government.</u>

8. The structure of the Mesopotamian government <u>changed</u> with the rise and fall of the successive <u>empires</u>.

9. As the Mesopotamian rule expanded, it became impossible for one ruler to govern both the <u>civil</u> and <u>religious</u> duties.

10. The first war in Mesopotamia (and possibly in history) happened during the Second Early Dynastic II when <u>Enmebaragesi</u> of Kish conquered <u>Elam</u> in 2700 B.C.E.

Empire Builders: Great Rulers of Mesopotamia

Sargon of Akkad entered history as the ruler of the world's first powerful empire, but he was much more than just a ruler. According to himself, Sargon had a humble beginning in life but was chosen by the gods to become king.

One of the main events that ensured Sargon's victory throughout all his conquests (and he conquered many Sumerian cities in his time) was his apparent support by the gods. He claimed to always do what the gods tell him to do – he doesn't rule himself but rules according to god's will.

Hammurabi of Babylon was a different kind of king, and this was clearly shown in his popularity. He introduced law concepts like the presumption of innocence and proof, both of which were new (but greatly appreciated) to the people. For the first time, people received punishment according to their social status – and, even more surprisingly, this did not include any privilege.

Ashurbanipal of Assyria was the last king wielding any significant power. Besides power over the region and his people, he was also concerned about leaving a legacy based on ancient cultural values. Unfortunately, only a fraction of what he left behind remained for future generations as everything else was destroyed during the reign of the Persian Empire.

Picture-Based Questions

1. The Ishtar Gate was built around 575 B.C.E. during the rule of Nebuchadnezzar II, one of the most famous kings of Babylonia. The gate was the main entrance to the city of Babylon and one of the eight gates guarding the empire's capital.

2. They were high-ranking officials, likely reporting directly to the king. You can tell this by their headgear, which almost looked like a crown – indicating they were just as powerful in the region they supervised as was the king on the empire level.

3. The list is called the Sumerian King List. Besides the names of the Sumerian rulers, it also has information about rulers of the neighboring regions and the length of all their reigns. It begins with the first king after the flood, referencing the flood myth, which was based on a mixture of mythology and real-life events occurring around two unpredictable rivers.

4. This was Enmebaragesi (also known as Mebaragsi), the king of Kish. He replaced the kings of Eridu, who ruled before the flood in 2900 B.C.E.

5. According to Sumerian beliefs, Eridu was founded by Enki, the god of wisdom, which meant it was the oldest city in the world. Order was first established in this city, and all other cities must follow the example of this order.

6. The cities founded during the Uruk period started to expand at the beginning of the Early Dynastic I period and continued until their population grew too large to be governed by one ruler.

7. Elam was the defeated party in the first war in recorded history. In 2700 B.C.E., emerging from the events of the Great Flood, Enmebaragesi of Kish launched an attack on Elam and was successful in securing victory over the nation's first battlefield enemy.

8. She was Kubaba of Kish, the wife of Enmebaragesi. It's unclear whether she made the list based on her accomplishments or her husband's deeds. Still, her name on the list as the only queen was a huge accomplishment on its own.

9. This was the moon god Nanna, the patron of Ur. Ur-Nammu built many sacred places in Nanna's honor, including the large ziggurat in the temple complex in Ur. Many of these had depictions of the god in this position, seated on the throne, holding the ring and the rod (the indicators of kingship).

10. The picture shows Ahura Mazda, the main deity of the Sassanian Empire, bestowing kingship to Ardashir I. The Sassanian rule lasted from 224 to 651 C.E.

Short Answer

1. Nebuchadnezzar II was perhaps the most ambitious ruler of Mesopotamian civilization. He expanded the Babylonian Empire, adding Jerusalem and Judah to its territories. He was also believed to have commissioned the Hanging Gardens of Babylon (although the gardens in question were never found).

2. Reigning from 745 - 727 B.C.E., Tiglath-Pileser III, the Assyrian king, made many advances in the empire's political system. He also improved the military tactics, making them more efficient in conquering the opponent.

3. After the Medes conquered Babylonia, the great empire was at risk of vanishing. Cyrus the Great defeated the Medes and took control over Babylonia, establishing the Persian Empire.

4. The main concept the early Mesopotamian government was based on was similar to a regular household in the region. The father was the head of the household, and everyone else was expected to obey his rules (the king was the absolute ruler, and everyone else was under his command).

5. After conquering the Sumerian city-states, Sargon established the administrative position of Citizen of Akkad. This position was awarded to trusted officials who were sent from Akkad to become the administrators, governors, priests, and priestesses of the cities.

6. Ur-Nammu was seen as similar to previous rulers, except fairer – perhaps because he claimed to be a god instead of a human guided by a deity. He was seen as a father figure who cared for his people.

7. Shulgi of Ur encouraged people to get a better education. He also improved roads and built more roadside gardens and inns. All of this made him more popular among the citizens who approved of a ruler who showed he cared about the people and not just the land.

8. During his reign, Hammurabi was known as the Builder of the Land – due to his efforts to improve the infrastructure of Mesopotamian cities.

9. Besides regulating unacceptable behaviors, the Code of Hammurabi also defined and considered social status. This

meant the people's status in society affected how they were treated before the law.

10. When an empire turned into a different one, this was accompanied by cultural and religious changes, too. For example, in the Assyrian Empire, the main god to worship was Ashur. Whereas during the Babylonian Empire, people worshiped Marduk.

Warfare and Diplomacy: Power Dynamics in Ancient Mesopotamia

In the early days, the only military strategies Mesopotamian city-states were interested in were the ones that allowed them to overpower another city-state. Trade with other civilizations had not started yet – but when it did, everything became more complicated.

Mesopotamia has many treasures, but natural resources were not among these. Trading and, more importantly, conquering other territories helped them secure these resources. This didn't always go as planned (or how the conquering ruler wished it would go).

One of the best examples of this is the rule of Sargon the Great, whose administrators had to subdue many rebellions after he conquered the Sumerian city-states. Some kings exiled people from conquered territories based on their religion.

The power dynamics between the civil and religious rulers were also interesting. Once these duties were no longer united, the king would share power with a religious leader, but this leader had to be appointed by him.

Other rulers are seen as good-natured and brave heroes, deities, and even father figures. These were the ones who learned from the previous mistakes. They had good relationships not only with their own people but also with surrounding civilizations.

Then came the kings who, once again, wanted to start conquering new territories. They disregarded the good connections, lost, and eventually caused the downfall of the last Mesopotamian Empire.

Chapter 6

Multiple Choice Questions

1. C. In ancient Mesopotamia, houses were often built from mud brick. This material was similar to what they used for the clay tablets. After extracting it from the riverbank, they shaped the

mud into brick form and dried it in the air (it's called sun-baking). The mud-brick walls kept the homes warmer in winter and cooler in the summer.

2. B. Before agriculture advanced and the cities began to grow, Mesopotamians lived in small settlements, hunted animals for food and clothes, and gathered greens for additional food resources.

3. A. The middle class of Mesopotamian society was the smallest in numbers. It was made up of merchants, craftsmen, and civil servants.

4. B. and C. Mesopotamians wore clothes made from wool and sheepskin. Women wore long dresses, while the men wore kilt-like skirts. In later periods, they would place metal accessories on their clothes or wear jewelry made from metal.

5. A. Daily life for most Mesopotamians depended on their occupation and social status. Those with a lower status spent their days working, while those in the upper levels had more time for fun activities, learning, etc.

6. C. Starting with Sargon the Great, all Mesopotamian kings were seen as divine messengers. According to the legends, when people needed something, kings of cities, regions, or empires could ask for it from the gods and goddesses, and they would receive it. A king's ability to conquer larger territories meant that they had a close connection to a deity.

7. B. Lesser priests and priestesses had the task of overseeing the sacred aspects of daily life in the temple complex. This included reading signs and omens and organizing and holding ceremonies and services.

8. A. The first Mesopotamian doctors were priestesses who saw sick or injured people outside the temples. They would see and try to cure everything from a toothache to broken bones. They learned how to use medicinal herbs, which came in handy when someone needed healing.

9. D. While social status was an important difference, the amount of free time and the money they earned was even more crucial for the merchants of the different social classes. Those who owned shops earned more money and didn't need to travel, so they had enough money and time to spend hours drinking beer with their

friends in the city.

10. B. In ancient Mesopotamia, all school teachers were scribes. They had the same education they were providing to their young students in the Tablet Houses.

True or False

1. False. Most scribes and scholars were men. Women were rarely given the opportunity to study writing. The only exceptions were the daughters of important administrators and kings, many of whom became priestesses and learned to write.

2. False. While some people moved to work in the city, many of them still worked in the fields and farms. The thriving Mesopotamian society was based on farming and agriculture, and it wouldn't have been able to grow without people working in the industry.

3. True. Laborers and farmers had to work hard, so their lives were harder, too. However, their work paid off, and some even moved up on the societal scale. More importantly, their work was essential for the growth of the Mesopotamian society.

4. True. Slaves were the lowest members of the Mesopotamian society. All slaves were owned by the king but could be sold and bought by any member of the upper class. Most slaves were people captured in battles and conquests of the nearby territories.

5. True. In larger cities, there were many artists, including poets, storytellers, potters, and sculptors. They showered people with religious-themed art or pieces honoring the past and present kings of Mesopotamia and the city itself.

6. True. Mesopotamian women had long hair, often wearing it in complicated braids. The men also had long hair and usually sported a full beard as well.

7. False. The lower classes couldn't afford to get candles for lighting. They would go to bed in the dark and often wake up in the dark, too, as they worked longer hours and had to get up early.

8. False. Besides adult men and women, children could also be slaves. Moreover, older children would often be given the same difficult tasks as adults. They worked in construction or road building. Skilled slaves (who were often war prisoners) worked as

helpers for accountants, jewelry makers, or teachers.

9. True. Mesopotamian men and women loved using perfume. They put on clothes and their bodies after bathing. Perfume making wasn't too hard (it only required steeping aromatic herbs in water and oil), and everyone who knew how to make good perfume could move up in society.

10. False. Mesopotamians never lived under a unified rule, not even during the height of the Akkadian Empire. Even when Upper and Lower Mesopotamian were united in the first millennia B.C.E., there were still some differences in the government of the two territories.

Fill-in-the-Blank

1. Mesopotamians used gold bars as a form of currency in their trade and economic transactions.

2. When the cities grew, more people were able to get jobs because there were a lot more duties and activities to do.

3. Mesopotamian societies were divided into different classes of people.

4. The top of the Mesopotamian hierarchy was occupied by the king.

5. The upper level of Mesopotamian society was made up of wealthy members, like priests, scribes, and high-level administrators.

6. Laborers and farmers belonged to the lower class.

7. Besides work, people in the larger towns and cities also found the opportunity for fun activities.

8. Both women and men wore makeup, especially in the upper classes.

9. Wealthier homes had windows to let in more sunlight and sesame oil lamps for additional lighting.

10. Ancient Mesopotamians would wash up and dress in clean clothes for the evening meal.

Picture-Based Questions

1. Marketplaces like this one, set up on the town square of Hit, were suitable for trading everything from animals to craft products. Merchants would also sell clothes, jewelry, food, and imported products. Once the trade happened, the amounts were written down by the assisting scribes.

2. The picture shows an Assyrian quartet playing music – a very important part of social life in ancient Mesopotamia. Besides religious ceremonies and functions, music was played for kings and other wealthy members of society, and even at homes where families gathered for the night.

3. This is an amulet, often worn on a necklace. Mesopotamians wore amulets as they believed that these objects were blessed by gods and would protect them from harm.

4. The picture shows the celebration of a royal bull hunt in the Assyrian Empire. Besides the king and other wealthy members of the society, musicians also attend the event. You can also see slaves around the royals, waiting for their orders.

5. Some women and men are wearing long robes. The women's robes have more layers and details than the men's. Older men usually wore longer robes falling to their ankles. Younger ones wore either a shorter robe or a pleated skirt.

6. This was a furniture panel made from wood and ivory. It often decorated beds, chests, and walls in wealthy Assyrian households.

7. They were chariot drivers. They drive kings and wealthy members of society to all functions, including battles, public speaking, and celebrations. Some would use chariot drivers just to go about their day in the city. Those who could afford to pay the drivers showed their status simply by riding around in a chariot.

8. She was Kubaba, the queen of the town of Kish. Before she became queen, Kubaba worked as a tavern keeper. She is one of the few non-male rulers of Mesopotamia, as most cities and towns were ruled by kings.

9. Mesopotamian children would often play a jump rope game named after the love goddess Ishtar. Besides ball games, this was the children's other favorite activity in good weather.

10. They were likely drinking beer, as this was most Mesopotamians drink of choice during the day. The wine was usually used for celebrations and among the wealthy. Beer, on the other hand, was a filling addition to everyone's midday meal.

Short Answer

1. Mesopotamians had different jobs in the cities. Besides priests and priestesses, they were scribes, soldiers, craftsmen, merchants,

laborers, and civil servants.

2. Mesopotamia was the land of few resources. Many essential resources were not available but could be obtained from other civilizations. Trading allowed Mesopotamians to advance their society.

3. They took advantage of the region's rich soil and water sources and developed a very efficient agriculture, beginning with the complex irrigation systems. This new technology allowed them to produce more food than required so their cities could grow.

4. Mesopotamian houses were rectangular and had a flat roof. The homes of the middle and upper-level members had two or three levels. People often slept on the roof during the hot summer nights.

5. Many enjoyed concerts and festivals, where they could see artists playing the flutes, harps, lyres, or drums. Others would participate in sports like wrestling, swimming, and boxing.

6. The typical meal consisted of bread and vegetable stew, both flavored with fresh, locally grown herbs. Sometimes, they would eat fish or, on special occasions, roasted lamb or mutton. Onions and grains were eaten with every meal, and the men would wash off their meals with a cup of beer or two.

7. Most Mesopotamian homes had simple furniture made of reeds and wood. The frames of their chairs looked similar to modern chairs. Homes on the upper level also had couches made of wood animal skin, decorated wooden chests, beds, and tables with metal finishing. The poor slept on reed mats and likely had no table, either.

8. Children play with toys that are very similar to modern toys. They had dolls, trucks, small building blocks, balls, hoops, and jump rope. In wealthy homes, girls also played with toy furniture pieces, while boys had toy bows and arrows.

9. Writing allowed the scribes to record everything they wanted to preserve for future generations. Once they saw how useful writing is, they started recording everything (which allowed future generations – including the modern ones – to see what life in ancient Mesopotamia looked like).

10. Besides sending them to school (which was typically run by the local temple), wealthy families would also use private tutors for their children. The tutors were very intelligent and educated themselves, and they could earn more money teaching than working as scribes and teachers in schools.

Chapter 7

Multiple Choice

1. C. The ziggurat was primarily used as a religious temple. Priests and priestesses would hold religious functions at the ziggurat, often praising or hoping to appease a god or goddess and earn their favor.

2. A. The first places of worship had elements decorated with animals and other natural motives. This indicates that the earliest civilization worshiped nature the most and had a great respect for the natural world.

3. As the settlements grew throughout the Uruk Period, more protective measures were needed around the city. Building wells with strategically placed watchtowers allowed the citizens to monitor who enters and leaves and keep everyone safe from a potential enemy.

4. B. Royal courts and palaces often had outer walls, too, for added protection of the royal family. The walls were decorated with religious-themed paintings. Sometimes, there were two walls, one around the palace and one massive defensive wall around the outer court.

5. C. The first anthropomorphic figures appeared during the Third Dynasty of Ur. They were decorations similar to early votive figures, except they were much larger and had large eyes. They were built by wealthy families in honor of their patron goddess or god.

6. A. One of the most famous Mesopotamian architectural structures still standing today is the Ishtar Gate of Babylon, commissioned by Nebuchadnezzar II in 575 B.C.E.

7. B. Builders and architects of ancient Mesopotamia wanted to mirror nature and the universe. They believed that the gods and goddesses created order in the universe because this established a balance. They wanted to replicate this order so people could

have balance in their lives, too.

8. D. While Mesopotamians are well known for their use of complex irrigation systems that reshaped the future of agriculture, the ziggurats, the use of mud brick, and decorations played just as big of a role in their architecture.

9. A. Besides the skills to make something useful and pleasing to the eye, building novel Mesopotamian structures also required plenty of imagination and thinking outside the box. Imagination allowed builders to design something unique, and thinking helped them create it even when it seemed impossible.

10. B. The Tower of Babel is known from the origin myth tied to the languages and biblical literature. Both of these claim that the Babylonians built the tower to show they could create something that would reach the heavens. To prevent this, God made workers speak different languages so they wouldn't understand each other (which made finishing the tower impossible).

Monuments to the Gods and Kings: The Architecture of Mesopotamia

Many of the famous Mesopotamian buildings were erected in honor of gods, goddesses, and mythical creatures. Each city, town, and settlement had its divine protector, to whom the locals prayed and expressed their gratitude.

Ziggurats are the most well-known worship monuments and probably the most notable ones, too, as some could reach over 300 feet in height. The massive structures required a lot of effort and imagination to complete – and that's without mentioning the immense amount of work that went into making the decorative elements.

Besides temples and traditional worship sites, some deities were honored with moments or decorations at the entrance of cities (for example, the Ishtar Gate) or palaces. The decorations were often made of colorful tiles, which took artists many hours to paint.

Lamassu, a protective deity/mythological creature, also had several moments and decorative elements built in their honor. Most of them originate from the Neo-Assyrian period when Mesopotamian architects were trying to reach back to their roots by honoring people's connections to nature while respecting the current gods.

True or False

1. True. As the Mesopotamian settlements grew, it became important for everything to have its place in the town or city. Over time, they found it easier to build everything in a predesigned grid layout – beginning a tradition that would shape architecture in coming civilizations.

2. True. Archeologists suggest that the first larger buildings made from mud-brick (including the 10,000-year-old Göbekli Tepe) were temples. There were no other signs of living activities in the area, which meant the place was likely considered sacred.

3. False. Between 5000 and 4100 B.C.E., Mesopotamians also built houses from rows of reed, except most of these were destroyed while many brick houses remained.

4. False. The clever Mesopotamians have already begun to build canals and aqueducts to improve agriculture during the Uruk Period. However, they further improved these during the Early Dynastic Period.

5. True. Art and architecture began to thrive even more after the kingship and priesthood were divided. The priests had more time and opportunity to study different topics – like writing, which also helped art and architecture improve in Mesopotamia.

6. False. Ur-Nammu commissioned the building of the Great Ziggurat of Ur, but the construction was never finished during his reign. His son, Shulgi of Ur, was the one who completed the structure, honoring his father's wishes.

7. True. Nabonidus, the last Babylonian king, made great efforts to restore the architectural wonders of previous empires. This included the reconstruction of the Ziggurat of Ur, which was destroyed during the rise of the Persian Empire.

8. True. Their shape and size made ziggurats perfect not only for religious functions but also for political events.

9. True. Archeological evidence suggests that other large gardens were built before the Babylonian Empire was even founded. One of these was the garden of the palace of Ashurbanipal, which is depicted on a decorative relief from the wall of the palace.

10. False. Decorative elements and furniture found in the ruins of Uruk indicate they were created in honor of the goddess Inanna.

Fill-in-the-Blank

1. The <u>irrigation</u> system was a key innovation that allowed Mesopotamians to control river water for irrigation.

2. The earliest temples had <u>rectangular</u> buildings laid out in a <u>circular</u> pattern and <u>T-shaped</u> pillars.

3. The Mesopotamians perfected the construction of ziggurats in the <u>Uruk</u> period.

4. <u>Architects</u> and <u>sculptors</u> made some of Mesopotamia's most memorable work during the thought of the Akkadian Empire.

5. Ur-Nammu built palaces and courts surrounded by <u>orchards</u> and <u>gardens</u>.

6. Shulgi of Ur continued his father's legacy by founding the first <u>roadside</u> <u>inns</u> with landscaped gardens.

7. Besides making the buildings look nicer, the intricate decorations on Mesopotamian buildings also showcased political, religious, and <u>social</u> ideas.

8. Like many other places of worship in Mesopotamia, the Ziggurat of Ur has several <u>stories</u> and is over 90 feet tall.

9. With its complex <u>patterns</u> and colorful <u>decorations</u>, Babylonian architecture art was a true representation of the civilization's cultural and monetary riches.

10. Since most other large Mesopotamian gardens were all built near large <u>buildings</u>, where there were walls, shade, and sufficient water resources, some believe that the Hanging Gardens of Babylon may have been built near the <u>palace</u> of Nebuchadnezzar.

Picture-Based Questions

1. These are the ruins of a ziggurat and temple in the city of Borsippa. The structure was once used to worship the Nabu, the god of scribes, wisdom, and literacy. Followers would gather around the priest or priestess and participate in the ceremony, which either praised Nabu or hoped to gain its favor (and not his anger).

2. Choga Mami is the site where the oldest irrigation canal was found. It was built around 6000 B.C.E., during the Ubaid Period. The settlement was established after the canal was dug

up, and there were sufficient water resources for agriculture and daily living.

3. Animal-themed plaques usually meant a deep respect for nature and the gods or divine creatures governing it. This plaque, in particular, depicts Mushussu, the mythical animal appearing in Babylonian literature. Its use in architectural decorations was meant to protect the home's inhabitants from their enemies.

4. This clay peg was used to make wall decorations. The sharp end could make precise carvings and patterns that would adorn outer walls. In wealthy homes, where there were outer and inner walls, sometimes, the inner walls were also decorated with carved patterns.

5. These small ceramic figurines are examples of fertility-themed art and architecture. They date back to the early days of urban Mesopotamia, around 4500 B.C.E.

6. The picture shows a votive vase decorated with an offering scene to Inanna (Ishtar), which means it was used in a temple dedicated to the goddess. Other gods, like Ea, for example, had similar objects (vases, plaques, registers, water basins, etc.) dedicated to them in their temples.

7. The picture shows the ruins in modern-day Iraq at the (possible) location of the Hanging Gardens of Babylon. Many argue that the gardens were not built in Babylon at all but in another city, possibly Nineveh.

8. The pegs were buried under a building's foundation. They had protective roles but also preserved the builder's name for future generations (like a modern-day signature on an art piece). The pegs from the picture are thought to originate from 2130 B.C.E., under the Temple of Ningirsu, in southern Mesopotamia.

9. The Chogha Zanbil ziggurat dates back to 1250 B.C.E. It was built by the king of Elam (modern-day Iran) and was later thought to be completely destroyed by Ashurbanipal in the 7th century B.C.E. However, parts of it were found during an excavation in the region.

10. The ruins belong to Tell Brak, a settlement dating back to around 4800 B.C.E. Tells were raised structures made from the accumulation of several small settlements. Tell Brak was destroyed and finally abandoned during the Assyrian rule around

1300 B.C.E.

Water Wizards: The Irrigation Systems of Mesopotamia

Living in the Fertile Crescent only meant that there was a sufficient water source nearby. To use this water in their fields, the Sumerians first had to dig canals between the Tigris and the Euphrates. These canals directed water from one river, ran across the fields, and brought the water to the other river.

The canals looked like modern war trenches, except the dirt that was dug up from them was left on the side. It was later used to bury the canal in strategic places and let the water flood the fields.

Later, Sumerians also created larger canals called levees, which could carry more water. Levees run perpendicular to the water surface and turn backward toward the land. The Sumerians enhanced this by placing reed walls and clay brick walls in the path of canals leading inland.

These innovative solutions allowed Mesopotamian settlements and later cities to thrive for several reasons. During dry weather, they could direct water to the field for irrigation. During flood season, they would redirect the water from the river, saving the crop-filled fields from ruin.

Kings had control over the irrigation system and could distribute water as they desired. Most city-states were built close to the river but on a hill – so they would be safe in flood season. The canals were dug around the cities, where farmers could use them on their fields and farms.

Short Answer

1. In the beginning, the Hanging Gardens of Babylon were the symbol of the rich and thriving status of the Babylonian Empire. It was built with a never-before-seen layout and structure, which was only possible through an architectural marvel other civilizations couldn't even imagine. Later, the gardens inspired many artists visiting from faraway lands, who incorporated this unique Mesopotamian motive in their artwork and culture.

2. Some examples of early Mesopotamian artwork include Göbekli Tepe, the oldest place of worship in the world, dating back to 10,000 B.C.E., or Çatalhöyük, the first city with urban construction, dating back to around 7500 B.C.E., or the similar city of Tell Brak, from 6500-5000 B.C.E.

3. By the early 21st century B.C.E., palaces had two large courtyards connected by a lavishly decorated audience hall (also known as a throne room). Around the outer courtyard were storage areas, workshops, and offices – whatever was needed in a given court. The residences of the royal family were around the well-protected inner courtyard.

4. The first was the practical purpose, but beyond this, people's relationship with deities also influenced the builders' work. What role the owner played in the society and what perspective they had on the world also affected what they wanted from the architect to accomplish.

5. The first thing Mesopotamians did was to ensure water could flow from the higher areas to the lower ones. They did this by building levees between the two rivers so those in the lower-laying areas could also grow crops.

6. Most regular homes were built from mud bricks dried in the sun. The mud bricks for temples, ziggurats, and other places of worship were typically dried in a kiln, which made them higher quality and more durable (perhaps this is why some are still standing).

7. A successful completion of the structure (and the subsequent public approval) was a wonderful opportunity for builders, architects, and artists to showcase their talents. Many of them gained recognition and a higher social status by building something unique and much admired by locals and visitors alike.

8. They held a ceremony to honor the deity that would be the patron of the building. Without the blessing of a patron god or goddess, the building wasn't considered complete, even if every brick and decorative element was in place.

9. This was to show that their ruler's authority came from the gods. It was a way to move a religious message into monuments honoring kings and heroes.

10. The Assyrians invented a technique of carving design motifs into standing stones and cliffs. It was later improved by the Persians but was still an innovative way to bring nature, religious motifs, and people closer together.

Chapter 8

Multiple Choice Questions

1. C. Sargon of Akkad was a true military leader. He conquered nearly all Sumerian settlements and city-states, brought them under his rule, and founded the world's first empire.

2. B. Imperialism began to thrive in south Mesopotamia after the conquests of Sargon the Great. It continued through the Babylonian Empire but was ultimately pushed back when the North conquered and united with the South.

3. D. The Stele of the Vultures monument celebrated their victory over Umma at Lagash in 2600 B.C.E. The stele was made in honor of Eannatum, king of Lagash. This was the first moment recording a military victory in history.

4. A. While he used the removal of the boundary stone as an excuse to avenge a transgression, Eannatum actually had other intentions when attacking his neighbor. Namely, the neighbors' land had better access to overland trade routes, and Eannatum wanted to take control of them.

5. B. The king didn't trust the loyalty of people in the freshly occupied cities. Kings like Sargon, who expected blind loyalty from people who just came under his rule, had every right to distrust the newcomers. Many freshly conquered territories organized protests against the new ruler, and the king's men had to step in to reestablish order.

6. C. The most significant improvement in Mesopotamian warfare was the composite bow. Introduced in the Akkadian Empire, the composite bow was made of bone and wood pressed and glued together and completed with sinew string. Unlike the bow previously used by the Sumerians, the composite bow was stronger and more accurate even at larger distances.

7. B. and C. When new, more effective tools, like the composite bow, were introduced, the armories weren't needed at the front line anymore. This included the heavy chariots that carried massive weapon loads to defend from the enemy's advance.

8. B. The king who took control over the Assyrian territories by conquering the Kingdom of Mitanni was Suppiluliuma I, the ruler of the Hittites between 1344 and 1322 B.C.E.

9. D. Tukulti-Ninurta I was the Assyrian ruler who defeated the Hittites at the Battle of Nihriya. Incredibly, in the same year (around 1245 B.C.E.), he also managed to conquer the holy city of Babylon. Later, he was killed for transferring the Babylonian treasures to the Assyrian treasury.

10. C. The Assyrians preferred siege warfare. They would have a special branch of engineers who would devise a strategy to attack and conquer the enemy territory.

Legendary Figures of Mesopotamian Warfare

Sargon of Akkad (Sargon the Great)

According to Mesopotamian mythology, Sargon of Akkad, whose name meant "true king," might be gifted by the gods to establish the world's first empire. To do this, he had to use power and military tactics that were unheard of in his time. His successors continued improving on his tactics. Their success lay in a strategy that involved more than the use of force or demand for obedience. They exerted their power by winning battles and striking fear in their enemy, but also by being just rulers and showing their respect for the gods.

Before Sargon rose to power, he studied the Sumerian tactics and learned what made them thrive in battle and as a civilization. While working as a cupbearer for the king of Kish, he saw the conflicts between Kish, Ur, and Uruk and waited until the best moment to make his move. Then, he organized a troop of soldiers loyal to him, who helped him overthrow the king of Kish.

Sargon continued to conquer toward the south, ultimately defeating Lugalzagesi, the king of Sumer, in 2334 B.C.E. With each conquest, he added to his troops the men from the cities he overtook. Once he took control over Sumer, he established a professionally trained army that would conquer many other city-states all the way up to modern-day Syria.

True or False

1. False. The Assyrian army used horses and donkeys to pull battle chariots, but they didn't use elephants. It was used against them by the Indians, and later, the Persians also started to use imported battle elephants to conquer their enemies.

2. False. The war between Sumer and Elam in 2700 B.C.E. was only the first one with recorded historical evidence. Ancient legends

and myths mention conflicts and battles that have likely happened in the 4th millennium B.C.E. and some even before.

3. True. Due to the uneven distribution of resources, rivers, and mountainous terrains, conflicts were common among Mesopotamian people. Everyone tried to secure resources, sometimes taking them away from others to ensure their survival.

4. True. Some records suggest that the largest city-states were in a constant state of warfare for up to 3 millennia. There were short periods of peace enforced by the victorious party, but these never lasted too long.

5. False. The oldest helmet in the world dates back to 2500 B.C.E. and was worn by a Sumerian commander. Archaeological records (carvings) suggest that people have worn headpieces in battles even before this.

6. True. In the Akkadian Empire, the administrators were loyal to the king of the empire, not to the citizens. This system was set up by Sargon and continued through the rule of his successors.

7. True. Between rivals, when one would invent a defensive tactic or weapon, the other would work to find an offensive countermove to emerge victorious. For example, after the metal helmets were invented, someone came up with more powerful battle axes that would pierce through the metal headgear.

8. False. Scribes had another important role in battles. Their task was to calculate how much force the troops would need to use to take down the enemy. For example, when they wanted to conquer a city, the scribes would determine the amount of force needed to break down the city walls. They also added to the defense strategy by determining how to build an offensive ramp.

9. False. Kings of the Ur period used very different ruling and conquering tactics. Some would follow Sargon's model, while others took a kinder approach, hoping to avoid dissatisfaction and quickly establish order in newly occupied territories.

10. True. The Babylonian treasures added significantly to the wealth of the Assyrian Empire. They were used to revive the economy and rebuild the military. It's possible that if it weren't for the treasures stolen from Babylon, the Assyrian Empire wouldn't have reached as high before or after the reign of Ashurnasirpal II.

Legendary Figures of Mesopotamian Warfare II
Hammurabi

Several hundred years later, in the 18th century B.C.E., the Amorite king Hammurabi still used Sargon's military model. Just like the Akkadian ruler, he established a professional fighting force as soon as he came to power. He also made allies, including Larsa, who helped him trump over the Elamites.

To gain more power, Hammurabi later allied himself with Larsa's rivals, conquering Uruk, Isin, Nippur, and finally Lagash. By this time, all Mesopotamian city-states were under his command, and he controlled them from Babylon.

Hammurabi also used a tactic he learned from his father, Sin-Muballit. When a city-state refused to surrender, he would either block its water supply or dam the canals, then flood the city just before he attacked. It was a brutal but highly effective tactic that worked perfectly. Even if he had to flood an entire city-state – he would later rebuild it.

Fill-in-the-Blank

1. The Battle of <u>Elam</u> was a significant conflict in Mesopotamian history involving the Babylonians and the Elamites.

2. In ancient Mesopotamia, armed conflicts were often recorded through <u>artwork</u> and cuneiform <u>inscriptions</u>.

3. Sometimes, wars were fought not between two nations but between their <u>patron</u> <u>gods</u>.

4. When several city-states or an empire went to a battle, each city-state had its own <u>militia</u>, which made organizing the strategy and <u>attack</u> much easier.

5. To maintain order, Sargon and his successors installed trusted <u>friends</u> and <u>family</u> <u>members</u> in important functions in all city-states.

6. People captured in battle could be executed but also <u>enslaved</u> or sometimes <u>freed</u> after a time.

7. The Akkadian Empire declined and was defeated by the <u>Gutians</u>, who were then not only conquered but also <u>exiled</u> from Mesopotamia during the third Ur period.

8. Hammurabi's empire was short-lived, but its conquerors, the <u>Kassites</u>, didn't fare much better either.

9. After the defeat of the Kassites, Mesopotamia went from one ruling power to another, beginning with the <u>Hittites</u> and followed by a series of <u>Assyrian</u> powers.

10. During a siege, the Assyrians used <u>mobile</u> <u>ladders</u> to get in and take control of a city.

Picture-Based Questions

1. The picture shows a classic combination of offense and defense tactics. The archers on the chargers are attacking the enemy while the rest of the soldiers are defending the line with their large shields.

2. He was Adad-Nirari III, the Assyrian king who ruled from 810 to 783 B.C.E. He was praying to the gods and goddesses for assistance and good outcomes in battle.

3. He was Shulgi of Ur, the first gentle ruler who tried to find a non-violent resolution to conflicts. On this seal, he is shown trying to find the balance between the advice of the god in front of him and the goddess behind him.

4. This vehicle only had two wheels, which means it belonged to the small war chariot category. The heavy chariots had four wheels to carry larger loads more easily.

5. The pictures show how much the empire grew by constantly raiding neighboring territories. This was a great testimony to the Akkadian rulers' skills and willingness to seek and introduce innovations in warfare and military tactics.

6. This is called the Golden Wig, the first metal helmet used by the Sumerians.

7. When the Assyrians under the rule of Sargon II came into conflict with the Urartu, very few people expected their victory. Yet, against all odds, Sargon's army cleverly defeats their enemy.

8. Assyrian archers covered all other members of the infantry, including the people who climbed the moats, lit fires underneath wooden gates, threw up ramps, etc.

9. He was Tiglath Pileser III, the Assyrian king who perfected the use of siege battle engines. He also had the skills and the courage to use whatever tactics it took to defeat the enemy. He always planned his campaigns well in advance, ensuring they would get him the results he wanted no matter how challenging a conquest

or defense was.

10. Ashurbanipal, the last Assyrian king known for his brilliant military moves, did not rebuild the cities he destroyed during his conquests. Instead, he relocated the entire population and left the cities and the fields empty.

Short Answer

1. Chariots gave Mesopotamians a huge advantage in battles. Those driving smaller chariots could move faster and attack the enemy's foot soldiers with arrows. By the time the enemy could react, they would drive away to a safer distance. Larger chariots also served as armories carrying weapons.

2. According to the Mesopotamians, gods wanted order. If a conflict arose, they would consult their patron deity and act depending on what signs they received back. If the omen said to attack the rival/enemy, it meant that the gods needed them to attack to restore order.

3. Sumerian soldiers had a wide range of weapons, including slings, daggers, bows, axes, javelins, and iron spears.

4. Sargon trained his militia to fight in a tight formation made of six men, where the front men were protected from the enemy by large shields. As the six-man group marched forward, behind them, archers and slingers opened fire.

5. Before their defeat by the Hittites, the Kingdom of Mitanni had strong control over the Assyrians. Once this threat was gone, Adad Nirari I organized his people and founded a new empire that would later take over all of Mesopotamia.

6. The unique battle Assyrians prided themselves on were wooden towers high several stories. They had four wheels, a top turret, and several battering rams at their bases.

7. They would choose one god and claim that everyone should follow this deity's will and disregard the others. This is very similar to how monotheistic religions work, which was definitely something new in a region ruled by polytheistic beliefs.

8. Sargon II took no credit for his victories, including his surprising victory over Urartu in 714 B.C.E. Instead, he claimed that his success was all the god Ashur's doing – as the god was guiding him in all decisions leading to the war.

9. While the Persian kings relied on the same military tactics as their predecessors, they made further improvements to it. For example, Cyrus II was able to form an even larger empire than the Assyrians with a professionally trained army and newer offense techniques that allowed him to move forward much faster.

10. According to a Mesopotamian myth, when Hammurabi destroyed the temple of Shamash, he ignored an inscription on the wall that was actually a curse. The curse threatened to unleash the wreath of gods on anyone who would desecrate the temple. Hammurabi did, and his alliance with the gods was seemingly severed because his empire was defeated soon after his death.

Chapter 9

Multiple Choice Questions

1. C. Wool was a major trading commodity. Wool and wool products for trade were prepared in temple workshops by slaves and young scribes.

2. B. The outposts were used for long-distance trade. As the trading routes expanded, merchants established outposts for trading in neighboring and faraway territories.

3. D. Mass-produced pottery, leather goods, jewelry, basketry, devotional figurines, and ivory carvings were all produced in temple workshops.

4. A. and B. Besides agricultural products, flax and dates were exported from Mesopotamia.

5. C. and D. With the development of the wheel and sail, transportation of goods became easier. Heavy bulk goods could travel by ox cart or be loaded onto riverboats.

6. B. Other than food items, Mesopotamia was rich in mud, clay, and reeds – all materials they used to build their cities.

7. A. After conquering vast territories, Hammurabi ordered the improvement of Mesopotamian infrastructure, earning the title "Builder of the Land." He was responsible for the construction of buildings where merchants could rest while traveling (roadside inns), store their products (warehouses), and conduct

their trade.

8. B. In Mesopotamia, local trade began in the Ubaid period, between 5000 and 4100 B.C.E. Mesopotamians relaxed early on that bartering what they had in surplus would help them get what they needed.

9. D. While Mesopotamians had trade routes to further distances much before this, trade with Egypt was only established in the Uruk Period.

10. C. Ziggurats were landmarks signaling larger cities. Larger cities meant bigger trading opportunities, so merchants would rather stop at ziggurats in Mesopotamia. They would see from the city farther away and know they'll have trading opportunities there.

True or False

1. True. The bartering system was a common trading method in ancient Mesopotamia. The concept of money wasn't invented yet, so trading one product for another was how everything changed hands.

2. True. The Assyrian merchants were a family business trading all over Mesopotamia and beyond. Only when the business expanded, and no one from the family was available to travel, they would sometimes hire people from other territories to trade there.

3. False. Besides local Mesopotamian products, the Assyrian traders transported and traded items they bought in other lands. For example, in Anatolia, they would sell tin they purchased farther east.

4. True. Mesopotamian cities established trade all up and down the Tigris and Euphrates rivers and into Anatolia (modern-day Turkey).

5. False. By the 3rd millennium, Mesopotamia trade expanded in all directions and across multiple neighboring and faraway territories.

6. False. In most cases, Mesopotamians preferred overland trade, even long distances. They would transport the goods with caravans using donkeys and similar load-bearing animals. They liked donkeys in particular because these animals can carry up to 150 pounds and travel on mountainous terrains where wheeled

carts had difficulty getting through.

7. False. Mesopotamia needed trade for most essential goods, including metals.

8. False. Despite the many social revolts that marked the Akkadian period, trade kept thriving. Sargon and his successors were always able to put down the uprising to ensure they wouldn't affect the empire's growth.

9. True. The Gutians failed to maintain the land and maritime trade at the Akkadian heights. Moreover, they allowed robbers to stalk the highways and frighten merchants away from the prospects of carrying valuable goods long distances.

10. True. At the turn of the 2nd millennium, the major Mesopotamian city-states under Shulgi's reign all seemed to have engaged in long-distance trade, which encouraged prosperity, economic stability, and the rebirth of the region's culture known as the Sumerian Renaissance.

Fill-in-the-Blank

1. The city of Ur was a major trading hub in ancient Mesopotamia.

2. By the time of the Assyrian Empire, Mesopotamia was exporting grains, textiles, pottery, cooking oil, jewelry, leather goods, and baskets and was importing gold from Egypt, tin from Persia, silver from Anatolia, pears and ivory from India, and copper from Arabia.

3. Overland trade routes went east toward the Zagros Mountains and all the way to present-day Afghanistan and Iran.

4. The Sea route extended through the Persian Gulf across the Arabian Sea to the Indus Valley.

5. Merchants and traders in early Mesopotamian cities began to form caravans for long-distance trading.

6. Copper and tin, used to make bronze, were especially important imports from foreign lands.

7. In the early days, merchants traveled on foot or used pack animals to transport goods.

8. Establishing trade routes to Egypt gave Mesopotamians access to imported wood and the novelty item, papyrus.

9. During the Early Dynastic III period and up to 2334 B.C.E., <u>Kish</u> and <u>Uruk</u> were the most dominant political and commercial powers.

10. A period of drought <u>during</u> the Gutian period halted the trade because it took away the <u>agricultural</u> surplus that was used for trading.

Picture-Based Questions

1. The seals were used to create clay tags for traded goods. They would be pressed into soft clay and then used to seal the mouths of jars.

2. The Anatolian merchants were the Assyrian's most frequent trading associates. They often brought wool textiles from the Assyrian merchants and sold them silver and natural resources.

3. Many times, jewelry was made from materials that couldn't be found in Mesopotamia. Craftsmen needed to import these to make jewelry, which they then sold back to the local and foreign markets.

4. This coin, the daric, was introduced by King Darius I between 522 and 486 B.C.E. His predecessor, Cyrus II, started using coins in trade, but their value wasn't standardized yet.

5. Clay tokens were a form of insurance within the barter system. The person who sold the goods would give the same number of tokens as the number of goods they sold, and the person who received them would count them to see if everything was in order. Tokens came in different shapes, depending on what product they accompanied.

6. These were the Amarna Letters, written around 1348-1320 B.C.E.

7. Dilmun, also known as the Land of the Gods by the Sumerians, was a central spot for trade with the Indus Valley civilization. Mesopotamian traders would travel to Dilmun and meet the Indus Valley traders carrying their local goods.

8. These unique figurines (sometimes called "lizard people") were popular in trade around 4000 B.C.E. Many of them, including this one, were made in the city of Ur, which was a major trading hub.

9. This early trade route reached up to the Zagros Mountains. Later on, Mesopotamians used more trade routes along the Tigris,

many of which went through Ashur (Assur).

10. These silver coils were used as currency. They were part of the complicated barter system, where they could be exchanged for heavier products, like barley.

The Role of Merchants in Mesopotamian Society

After a successful career, merchants became very influential in Mesopotamian society, but the road to this position was demanding. They would have to learn to secure goods (which sometimes meant lots of traveling), bring them to bazaars, and deal with haggling customers.

The customers themselves were traders from other regions, sometimes faraway lands, which produced something that couldn't be found elsewhere. From land routes, trading was transferred to boats, as the Tigris and the Euphrates were quite handy transportation routes.

Traders were skilled in organizing, gathering information, making connections, and, last but not least, accounting. With the ever-complicating barter system, they needed to have superb math skills. Alternatively, if a merchant owned their business, they could have hired scribes to conduct the accounting tasks, and they would only have to focus on other aspects of their business.

After bartering with clay tokens, metal coils, and other easy-to-transport materials, the invention of the coin was a much-welcomed change. Being able to pay for something with coins made a trade (and the merchant's life) much easier.

Short Answer

1. The Tigris and Euphrates provided more than enough resources for the nearby settlements. Southern Mesopotamia, in particular, produced agricultural products in surplus but could trade these for resources lacking in the land (metals, timber, etc.).

2. Long-distance traders would travel to far away cities, where they would pay a tax to the city administrators. In exchange, they could live in a city for a short period and trade with the locals and merchants who came from other territories.

3. Local trade allowed people living in the countryside to buy tools made in the city and the people in the city to purchase food made by people in the country.

4. For overland trade, Mesopotamians used animals, and animals pulled sleds. On the water, they transported goods via oar-

powered boats or sailboats.

5. Pavement was nonexistent, so Merchants would have to travel on dirt roads. They didn't have bridges to cross the water, so they would have to go around, which meant losing precious time. They might have attempted to cross the water on a ferry, but this still meant spending time dismantling and unpacking the cart. If they didn't want to waste time, they would hire boats, which was costly. They would also have to fear thieves or hire security guards to accompany them.

6. When Sargon established the Akkadian Empire and brought all city-states under one unified administration, he eliminated the rivalry between the cities. Prices and trading practices became standardized, ensuring fair commerce and equal opportunities to grow for all regions.

7. Trade began to thrive under Shulgi's rule. Shulgi of Ur standardized timekeeping, calendar, weights, and measures, enabling trade to work uniformly in every part of his kingdom.

8. When the Amorites came to rule and took control of trading, everything was a little chaotic (the Amorites lived in small settlements, and there was little constant in their trading practices). As an Akkadian king, Hammurabi conquered and unified the settlements and established a cohesive system once again.

9. Between 1500-1200 B.C.E., the Club of the Great Powers oversaw and regulated international trade. The club included Assyria, Alashiya, Arzawa, Babylonia, Egypt, Hatti (Kingdom of the Hittites), and Mitanni.

10. The more goods merchants began to trade, the more complicated the barter system became. Grains, clay figures, precious metals, and other goods were used as tokens, and keeping up with them all became very time-consuming. Some believe that it was easier to write down what someone bought and sold until they paid it off than to remember the barter combinations.

Chapter 10

Multiple Choice Questions

1. A. The concept of zero was unknown before the Mesopotamians. Rooted in a deep respect for nature and the order-loving gods, the Mesopotamians came up with the concept that it could be anything, from nothing to everything.

2. B. The lunar calendar – which modern calendars are based on – was developed based on Mesopotamian observations of the lunar cycles.

3. C. Mesopotamians created complex mathematical concepts, including the base-60 number system, which is used in geometry.

4. B. Irrigation allowed the ancient people to grow their own crops and feed their animals. This is how they were able to make the shift from a nomadic hunter-gatherer lifestyle to a stable society where people remained and built their future in the same place.

5. D. Mesopotamia "borrowed" many technological solutions from its neighbors, and vice versa. By exchanging their innovative technologies, the different civilizations contributed to each other's growth, helping shape future societies.

6. A. and C. Money and standardized weights and measures were crucial for the development of modern trading and monetary systems.

7. D. The wheel was one of the most transformative inventions in mankind's history. The Mesopotamian principle of the wheel is still used in modern vehicle technology.

8. B. Mesopotamians had a holistic approach to health, integrating physical and spiritual well-being – similar to popular alternative medicine approaches.

9. A. Congestion (which many modern cities face) was a new and very serious issue for the Mesopotamians in the quickly growing cities. The more people moved to larger cities, the more space they had to create for them.

10. B. Composite bow was a significant invention in Mesopotamian warfare. In ancient times, the impact of its introduction in warfare was similar to the first use of gunpowder in modern weapons. It was an innovative solution that inspired many new

techniques for future generations of warfare.

True or False

1. True. The sexagesimal system, developed in 3100 B.C.E., is still in use today. It was slightly modified to fit the actual principles, but it's still a great way to measure angles and time.

2. True. Many civilizations adopted cuneiform writing and used it to convey their language and ideas. It was a stepping stone for the evolution of communication through the many millennia afterward.

3. False. Mesopotamians were great astronomers. Their catalog of stars and other heavenly objects helped modern scientists map the skies and make significant discoveries in the solar system.

4. True. The impossibly tall ziggurats and the gardens that required plenty of imagination and ingenuity to build and maintain are just some of the Mesopotamian architectural marvels that leave even modern artists and builders in awe.

5. False. Mesopotamian pottery, reliefs, and sculptures showcase incredible creativity, which influenced artists across all cultures.

6. False. Mesopotamian lore has many cues about ancient civilizations. Moreover, it's a collection of shared heritage for modern civilizations, helping explain mysteries and innovations that often occurred by leaps and bounds.

7. True. By engaging in trade with neighboring regions, Mesopotamia was one of the first civilizations to develop a trade system beyond its borders.

8. False. While Mesopotamian societies were largely monarchical, some elements of democratic principles, such as councils of elders and assemblies, were present. These early forms of collective decision-making provided a blueprint for later democratic systems.

9. True. The reason behind the Mesopotamians' successful growth and development is their efficient urban planning. They focused on sustainability and reasonable use of available resources. Through trading, the last of available resources grew, but Mesopotamians kept focusing on avoiding overuse.

10. True. Mesopotamia was a major hub for learning and education. They created schools and encouraged education, particularly for

scribes, laying the foundation for modern educational systems.

Fill-in-the-Blank

1. The <u>Hammurabi</u> Code, one of the oldest law codes, influenced modern legal systems.

2. The <u>Epic of Gilgamesh</u> still influences contemporary literature and storytelling.

3. The Mesopotamians made significant advances in the fields of <u>science</u>, which have impacted modern disciplines.

4. Modern agriculture uses canal systems and levees similar to those used by the Mesopotamians in the fields between the Tigris and the Euphrates.

5. The <u>Phoenician</u> alphabet, which evolved from the <u>cuneiform</u> script, was the prototype of the alphabet used in many languages today.

6. Many biblical tales, like the story of the <u>Great Flood</u>, have parallels in Mesopotamian lore, reflecting shared cultural values.

7. The concept of the <u>sovereign state,</u> where life is regulated by laws, can be traced back to the Mesopotamian civilization.

8. Many principles of Mesopotamian medicine, including the unique <u>diagnostic</u> process and the use of <u>natural</u> <u>remedies</u>, can be found in modern healthcare practices.

9. Mesopotamia's development of urban infrastructure, canals, buildings, roads, and trade routes are early examples of <u>urban planning</u>.

10. The power of <u>community</u> was another Mesopotamian legacy for modern societies.

Picture-Based Questions

1. The designers of the Guggenheim Museum in New York City were inspired by the design of the ziggurats, including the steep steps of the outer architectural layout.

2. This number system was used by the Sumerians before the invention of zero. In this early cuneiform script, they didn't have the sign or even the concept of zero (or nothing, as they called it).

3. The name you probably know this story by is the <u>Epic of Gilgamesh.</u> Interestingly enough, the pot was found in a region outside Mesopotamia. It proves that the influence of

Mesopotamian mythology was far-reaching, and heroes like Gilgamesh were and are known across the world.

4. The painter, Lydia Etheldreda Birch, was inspired by Mesopotamian riverside agriculture. The painting was created in 1875, over 6 millennia after a scene like this likely happened in ancient Mesopotamia.

5. Iraqi artist Dia Azzawi often drew inspiration from ancient Mesopotamian art and letters in his work. He is one of the many artists from the Arab Moderns movement who were inspired by ancient Middle and Near Eastern cultures.

6. This is the popular Bible Encyclopedia, the dictionary that defines and explains all religious terms, including biographical, geographical, historical, archaeological, and doctrinal themes.

7. All of these creatures are Mesopotamian hybrid beings said to have incredible powers and sometimes a divine essence. They appeared in clay tablets, immortalized by the Mesopotamian scribes and artists.

8. The constellation in the lower part of the picture, the Mush-Snake and a Raven, is pictured in two Babylonian clay tablets.

9. Many of the modern irrigation systems, including this one, were inspired by Mesopotamian watering techniques.

10. The building is made of bricks – a Mesopotamian invention. While modern bricks aren't made of air-dried clay patches anymore, they are still a crucial element of architecture.

Short Answer

1. Mesopotamian mythology influenced the literature of other civilizations in ancient times. All of these (including the original Mesopotamian myths) kept inspiring modern writers to create unique pieces. Modern literature and media often reach back to the tales of ancient gods and heroes, using them as examples of courage and growth.

2. Mesopotamia thrived on a model of market economy, where gods and services could be exchanged. This often involved complex economic interactions, which have slowly evolved into the contemporary economic and currency systems.

3. From the Akkadian Empire onward, the Mesopotamian concept of governance relied on a centralized power. The unified rule not

only defined boundaries (another useful concept for modern societies) but also eliminated rivalries between the cities under the same rule.

4. The legacy of Mesopotamian technology is evident in various fields. From the basic wheel to complex architectural techniques, these ancient innovations have been developed and refined over millennia, leading to the advanced technologies we use today.

5. Mesopotamians used minerals and herbs to treat illnesses, often recording their treatments. They also performed simple surgeries, which they also recorded. Their records and knowledge gave the foundation for modern medical literature.

6. Mesopotamians were masters of adaptation. They created a civilization in a very dry and resource-void region (which kept becoming even drier over time) by simply learning how to use the resources they had. In modern times, where people are dealing with disappearing resources, looking into how ancient civilizations adapted to this can help find solutions for sustainable living.

7. Mesopotamians had a passion for research, structured learning, and, fortunately for modern generations, the preservation of knowledge in libraries. These have also influenced contemporary education systems where people are encouraged to pursue knowledge and preserve it for others.

8. Modern living is all about making life simple and better. This is the same principle Mesopotamians were governed by. Each of their inventions is meant to improve something and make people's lives better. The following generation was inspired by these efforts, and they made their own to continue creating a better world – just as people do today.

9. Besides growing food, Mesopotamians also had to learn how to store it. After all, this was the first time they had to store an amount larger than what they could carry for a longer trip.

10. By mastering the basic mathematical operations, Mesopotamians learned how to keep accurate records of everything. They passed down their knowledge to future generations, leading to a transformative innovation in recordkeeping.

The Lasting Impact of Mesopotamian Myths and Stories

Like many other ancient lore, Mesopotamian myths and stories are based on religious themes. However, the deities appearing in Mesopotamian mythology are far more diverse.

Based on the archeological findings of texts, carved images, and art pieces tied to its legends, Mesopotamia mythology shows a much greater part of a shared heritage. By the height of the Babylonian Empire, Mesopotamia was a true melting pot of cultures. Yet, the growing pantheon of deities was kept alive in myths and stories just as it was when their numbers were smaller.

This diversity and legacy inspired many contemporary artists, builders, and even scientists to not only look into the background of the myths and stories but also use them in their own creations.

The religious aspects of Mesopotamian mythology were often adopted into other religions, where they kept on living and being passed down through generations. For the same reason, you can find religious ideas, concepts, and explanations for earthly events that sound very similar to ancient Mesopotamian myths.

If you enjoyed this book, a review on Amazon would be greatly appreciated because it would mean a lot to hear from you.

To leave a review:

1. Open your camera app.
2. Point your mobile device at the QR code.
3. The review page will appear in your web browser.

Thanks for your support!

Check out another book in the series

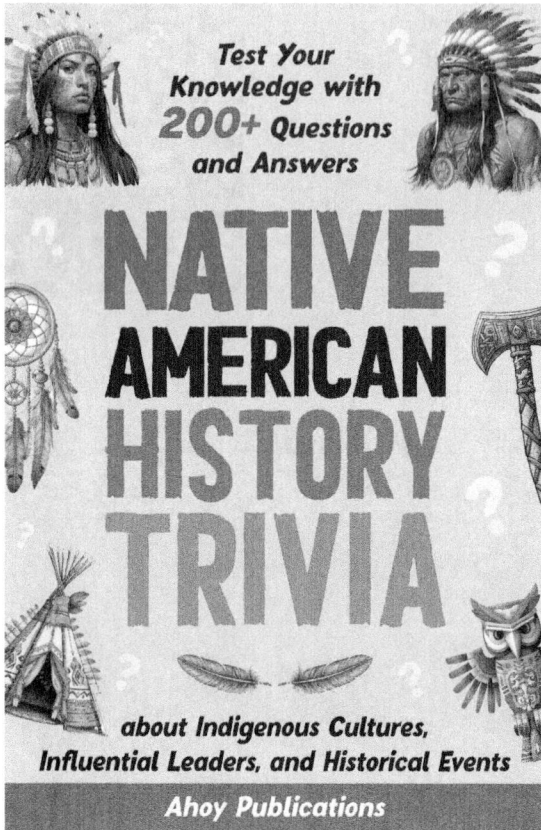

Test Your Knowledge with 200+ Questions and Answers

NATIVE AMERICAN HISTORY TRIVIA

about Indigenous Cultures, Influential Leaders, and Historical Events

Ahoy Publications

Welcome Aboard, Check Out This Limited-Time Free Bonus!

Ahoy, reader! Welcome to the Ahoy Publications family, and thanks for snagging a copy of this book! Since you've chosen to join us on this journey, we'd like to offer you something special.

Check out the link below for a FREE e-book filled with delightful facts about American History.

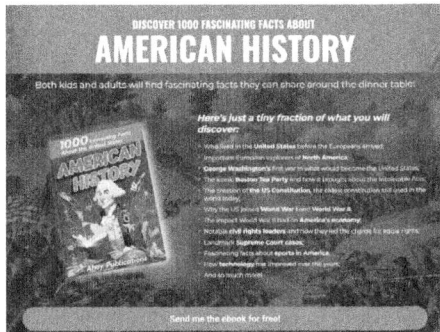

But that's not all - you'll also have access to our exclusive email list with even more free e-books and insider knowledge. Well, what are ye waiting for? Click the link below to join and set sail toward exciting adventures in American History.

Access your bonus here
https://ahoypublications.com/
Or, Scan the QR code!

References

admin. (2024, February 13). Mesopotamia's Legacy: Shaping Today's World. SOCIALSTUDIESHELP.COM. https://socialstudieshelp.com/mesopotamias-legacy-shaping-todays-world/

Ancient Mesopotamian Gods and Goddesses List of deities. (2019). Upenn.edu. http://oracc.museum.upenn.edu/amgg/listofdeities/

Andrée Herdner. (1950). Samuel Noah Kramer. – Schooldays: A Sumerian Composition relating to the Education of a Scribe. Syria. Archéologie, Art et Histoire, 27(3), 366–366.

Basic misconceptions about Mesopotamian mythology. (2019). Tumblr. https://vamavuandadu.tumblr.com/post/690421729604059136/basic-misconceptions-about-mesopotamian-mythology

Butt, A., Tabassum, P., & Saeed Imran, F. (2023). EXPLORING THE MESOPOTAMIAN TRADE (C.6000-539 BCE): TYPES, ORGANIZATION, AND EXPANSION. Palarch's Journal of Archaeology of Egypt/Egyptology, 20(1), 241–261.

Cartwright, M. (2018, July 27). Hanging Gardens of Babylon. World History Encyclopedia. https://www.worldhistory.org/Hanging_Gardens_of_Babylon/

Cataliotti, J. (2019). Mesopotamian Trade Routes & Transportation | Study.com. Study.com. https://study.com/academy/lesson/mesopotamian-trade-routes-transportation.html

Ducksters. (2019a). Ancient Mesopotamia: Daily Life. Ducksters.com. https://www.ducksters.com/history/mesopotamia/daily_life_in_mesopotamia.php

Ducksters. (2019b). Ancient Mesopotamia: Famous Rulers of Mesopotamia. Ducksters.com.

https://www.ducksters.com/history/mesopotamia/famous_rulers_of_ancient_mesopotamia.php

Hays, J. (2023). Ancient Mesopotamian Deities: Evolution, Meaning, Images | Middle East And North Africa – Facts and Details. Factsanddetails.com. https://africame.factsanddetails.com/article/entry-48.html

History for Kids. (2020). Daily Life of Mesopotamia Facts for Kids. History for Kids. https://www.historyforkids.net/daily-life-of-mesopotamia.html

History on the Net. (2014, September 19). Mesopotamia Trade: Merchants and Traders. History on the Net; Salem Media. https://www.historyonthenet.com/mesopotamia-trade-and-merchants

HISTORY.COM EDITORS. (2018, August 21). Mesopotamia. History; A&E Television Networks. https://www.history.com/topics/ancient-middle-east/mesopotamia

Irrigation System in Ancient Mesopotamia. (2023). https://www.athensjournals.gr/reviews/2023-5687-AJHIS.pdf

Khan Academy. (2019). Cuneiform. Khan Academy; Khan Academy. https://www.khanacademy.org/humanities/ancient-art-civilizations/ancient-near-east1/the-ancient-near-east-an-introduction/a/cuneiform

Khan Academy. (n.d.). Ancient Mesopotamian civilizations (article). Khan Academy. https://www.khanacademy.org/humanities/world-history/world-history-beginnings/ancient-mesopotamia/a/mesopotamia-article

Kiger, P. J. (2020, November 10). How Mesopotamia Became the Cradle of Civilization. History; A&E Television Networks. https://www.history.com/news/how-mesopotamia-became-the-cradle-of-civilization

Kordas, A., Lynch, R. J., Nelson, B., & Tatlock, J. (2023, April 19). 3.2 Ancient Mesopotamia - World History Volume 1, to 1500 | OpenStax. Openstax.org. https://openstax.org/books/world-history-volume-1/pages/3-2-ancient-mesopotamia

Legacy of Mesopotamia and Its Greatest Influence on Modern Civilization - Free Essay Example - Edubirdie. (2023). Edubirdie. https://edubirdie.com/examples/legacy-of-mesopotamia-and-its-greatest-influence-on-modern-civilization/

Mark, J. (2011a, February 23). Inanna's Descent: A Sumerian Tale of Injustice. World History Encyclopedia. https://www.worldhistory.org/article/215/inannas-descent-a-sumerian-tale-of-injustice/

Mark, J. (2011b, February 25). The Mesopotamian Pantheon. World History Encyclopedia. https://www.worldhistory.org/article/221/the-mesopotamian-pantheon/

Mark, J. (2014, April 15). Daily Life in Ancient Mesopotamia. World History Encyclopedia; World History Encyclopedia. https://www.worldhistory.org/article/680/daily-life-in-ancient-mesopotamia/

Mark, J. (2018, May 2). Assyrian Warfare. World History Encyclopedia. https://www.worldhistory.org/Assyrian_Warfare/

Mark, J. (2022, November 17). Cuneiform. World History Encyclopedia. https://www.worldhistory.org/cuneiform/

Mark, J. J. (2022, November 22). Trade in Ancient Mesopotamia. World History Encyclopedia. https://www.worldhistory.org/article/2114/trade-in-ancient-mesopotamia/

Mark, J. J. (2023a, February 13). Mesopotamian Warfare. World History Encyclopedia. https://www.worldhistory.org/Mesopotamian_Warfare/

Mark, J. J. (2023b, February 22). Mesopotamian Art and Architecture. World History Encyclopedia. https://www.worldhistory.org/Mesopotamian_Art_and_Architecture

Mrdonn. (2019). Ancient Mesopotamia Commerce and Money - Mesopotamia for Kids. Mrdonn.org. https://mesopotamia.mrdonn.org/commerce.html

Nedelcu, J. (2024). Mesopotamian Irrigation. http://www.giftednassau.com/uploads/1/0/1/4/101418208/mesopotania_irrigation.pdf

Popova, M. (2017, February 2). The Invention of Zero: How Ancient Mesopotamia Created the Mathematical Concept of Nought and Ancient India Gave It Symbolic Form. The Marginalian; The Marginalian. https://www.themarginalian.org/2017/02/02/zero-robert-kaplan

Rattini, K. (2019a, April 22). Hammurabi—facts and information. Culture. https://www.nationalgeographic.com/culture/article/hammurabi

Rattini, K. (2019b, June 18). King Sargon of Akkad—facts and information. Culture. https://www.nationalgeographic.com/culture/article/king-sargon-akkad

Salem Media. (2024, August 7). Daily Life in a Mesopotamian City: What Exactly Was It Like?" History on the Net © 2000-2024. https://www.historyonthenet.com/daily-life-in-a-mesopotamian-city

Spar, I. (2019). Gilgamesh. Metmuseum.org. https://www.metmuseum.org/toah/hd/gilg/hd_gilg.htm

Terradas, J. (2018, August 21). Still between the Tigris and the Euphrates - Blog CREAF. Creaf Blog. https://blog.creaf.cat/en/knowledge/still-between-the-tigris-and-the-euphrates/

van der Crabben, J. (2023, June 12). World History Encyclopedia. World History Encyclopedia. https://www.worldhistory.org/collection/167/mesopotamia-agriculture--innovations/

What is the Architecture of Mesopotamia? | Design Ideas for the Built World. (2017, November 8). Design Ideas for the Built World. Design Ideas for the Built World. https://caddetailsblog.com/post/what-is-the-architecture-of-mesopotamia

Where is The North. (2024). Architecture of Mesopotamia- Characteristics With Case Studies. Whereisthenorth.com. https://www.whereisthenorth.com/article/architecture-of-mesopotamia--characteristics-with-case-studies

Woods, C. (2024). Writing and Literature: Before Islam, Christopher Woods. Uchicago.edu. http://teachmiddleeast.lib.uchicago.edu/historical-perspectives/writing-and-literature/before-islam/framing-the-issues/issue-02.html

Image References

[1] Osama Shukir Muhammed Amin FRCP(Glasg), CC BY-SA 4.0 <https://creativecommons.org/licenses/by-sa/4.0>, via Wikimedia Commons: https://commons.wikimedia.org/wiki/File:Summary_account_of_silver_for_the_governor,_c._25 00_BCE._By_this_stage_of_cuneiform_writing,_the_reed_strokes_are_fully_wedge-shaped_and_the_writing_could_convey_the_Sumerian_language_in_full._Probably_from_Shuru ppak_(Tell_Fara),_Iraq.jpg

[2] Osama Shukir Muhammed Amin FRCP(Glasg), CC BY-SA 4.0 <https://creativecommons.org/licenses/by-sa/4.0>, via Wikimedia Commons: https://commons.wikimedia.org/wiki/File:Sumerian_votive_wall_plaque_with_3_registers_and_a _cuneiform_text,_from_Khafajah,_Iraq,_c._2600-2370_BCE._Iraq_Museum.jpg

[3] Hardnfast, CC BY 3.0 <https://creativecommons.org/licenses/by/3.0>, via Wikimedia Commons: https://commons.wikimedia.org/wiki/File:Ancient_ziggurat_at_Ali_ Air_Base_Iraq_2005.jpg

[4] The original uploader was Jolle at Catalan Wikipedia., CC BY-SA 3.0 <http://creativecommons.org/licenses/by-sa/3.0/>, via Wikimedia Commons: https://commons.wikimedia.org/wiki/File:Sharkalisharri.png

[5] Classical Numismatic Group, Inc. http://www.cngcoins.com, CC BY-SA 3.0 <http://creativecommons.org/licenses/by-sa/3.0/>, via Wikimedia Commons: https://commons.wikimedia.org/wiki/File:KINGS_of_MACEDON._Alexander_III_%27the_Gr eat%27._336-323_BC.jpg

[6] Mapa_Tercera_Dinastia_de_Ur.svg: Create Derivative work: Chaim The Bipolar, CC BY-SA 3.0 <https://creativecommons.org/licenses/by-sa/3.0>, via Wikimedia Commons: https://commons.wikimedia.org/wiki/File:Map_of_Ur_III.svg

[7] Enyavar, CC BY-SA 4.0 <https://creativecommons.org/licenses/by-sa/4.0>, via Wikimedia Commons: https://commons.wikimedia.org/wiki/File:Ancient_Near_East_1600BC.svg

[8] https://commons.wikimedia.org/wiki/File:Nimrud_-_Assyrian_helmets.png

[9] Osama Shukir Muhammed Amin FRCP(Glasg), CC BY-SA 4.0 <https://creativecommons.org/licenses/by-sa/4.0>, via Wikimedia Commons: https://commons.wikimedia.org/wiki/File:Sargon_II,_Iraq_Museum_in_Baghdad.jpg

[10] Fredarch, CC BY-SA 3.0 <http://creativecommons.org/licenses/by-sa/3.0/>, via Wikimedia Commons: https://commons.wikimedia.org/wiki/File:Nineveh_Adad_gate_exterior_entrance_far2.JPG

[11] Osama Shukir Muhammed Amin FRCP(Glasg), CC BY-SA 4.0 <https://creativecommons.org/licenses/by-sa/4.0>, via Wikimedia Commons https://commons.wikimedia.org/wiki/File:God_Ea.jpg

[12] Metropolitan Museum of Art, CC0, via Wikimedia Commons https://commons.wikimedia.org/wiki/File:Standing_Male_Worshiper.jpg

[13] Fred Wierum, CC BY-SA 4.0 <https://creativecommons.org/licenses/by-sa/4.0>, via Wikimedia Commons https://commons.wikimedia.org/wiki/File:Anzu_wyliei.jpg

[14] https://commons.wikimedia.org/wiki/File:Ashur_symbol_Nimrud.png

[15] https://commons.wikimedia.org/wiki/File:The_Pink_Fairy_Book_-_p113.png

[16] Roland E. Laffitte, CC BY-SA 4.0 <https://creativecommons.org/licenses/by-sa/4.0>, via Wikimedia Commons https://commons.wikimedia.org/wiki/File:GU.AN.NA_RL.jpg

[17] https://commons.wikimedia.org/wiki/File:Marriage_of_Inanna_and_Dumuzi.png

[18] Osama Shukir Muhammed Amin FRCP(Glasg), CC BY-SA 4.0 <https://creativecommons.org/licenses/by-sa/4.0>, via Wikimedia Commons https://commons.wikimedia.org/wiki/File:God_Enlil,_seated,_from_Nippur,_Iraq,_1800-1600_BCE._Iraq_Museum.jpg

[19] https://commons.wikimedia.org/wiki/File:Fragment_Bau_Louvre_AO4572.jpg

[20] https://commons.wikimedia.org/wiki/File:Marduk_and_pet.svg

[21] Internet Archive Book Images, No restrictions, via Wikimedia Commons https://commons.wikimedia.org/wiki/File:The_ancient_East_(1914)_(14594191287).jpg

[22] Astroskiandhike, CC BY-SA 4.0 <https://creativecommons.org/licenses/by-sa/4.0>, via Wikimedia Commons: https://commons.wikimedia.org/wiki/File:Fertile_Crescent.svg

[23] https://commons.wikimedia.org/wiki/File:Hero_lion_Dur-Sharrukin_Louvre_AO19862.jpg

[24] رديف بلال, CC BY-SA 4.0 <https://creativecommons.org/licenses/by-sa/4.0>, via Wikimedia Commons https://commons.wikimedia.org/wiki/File:%D8%A7%D9%87%D9%88%D8%A7%D8%B1_%D8%A7%D9%84%D8%B9%D8%B1%D8%A7%D9%82_._%D8%A7%D9%84%D8%AC%D8%A8%D8%A7%D9%8A%D8%B4_06.jpg

[25] https://commons.wikimedia.org/wiki/File:Ea_(Babilonian)_-_EnKi_(Sumerian).jpg

[26] https://commons.wikimedia.org/wiki/File:Place_V_1867_III_Plate_43_6_(extract3).jpg

[27] Şenol zümrüt, CC BY-SA 4.0 <https://creativecommons.org/licenses/by-sa/4.0>, via Wikimedia Commons https://commons.wikimedia.org/wiki/File:Hazar_G%C3%B6l%C3%BC_hazar_Baba_kayak_merkezinden_g%C3%B6r%C3%BCn%C3%BCm%C3%BC.jpg

[28] No machine-readable author provided. Kmusser assumed (based on copyright claims). CC BY-SA 2.5 <https://creativecommons.org/licenses/by-sa/2.5>, via Wikimedia Commons https://commons.wikimedia.org/wiki/File:Tigr-euph_de.png

[29] Near_East_topographic_map-blank.svg: Sémhurderivative work: Zunkir, CC BY-SA 3.0 <https://creativecommons.org/licenses/by-sa/3.0>, via Wikimedia Commons https://commons.wikimedia.org/wiki/File:Basse_Mesopotamie_DA.PNG

[30] GFDL, CC BY-SA 3.0 <https://creativecommons.org/licenses/by-sa/3.0>, via Wikimedia Commons https://commons.wikimedia.org/wiki/File:Mesopotamia-Indus.jpg

[31] Metropolitan Museum of Art, CC0, via Wikimedia Commons https://commons.wikimedia.org/wiki/File:Cuneiform_tablet-_hymn_to_Marduk_MET_DP360674.jpg

[32] Mary Harrsch, CC BY 2.0 <https://creativecommons.org/licenses/by/2.0>, via Wikimedia Commons https://commons.wikimedia.org/wiki/File:Babylonian_cuneiform_tablet_with_a_map_from_Nippur_1550-1450_BCE.jpg

[33] Metropolitan Museum of Art, CC0, via Wikimedia Commons https://commons.wikimedia.org/wiki/File:Cuneiform_tablet-_student_exercise_tablet_MET_DP360672.jpg

[34] See page for author, CC0, via Wikimedia Commons https://commons.wikimedia.org/wiki/File:Ritual_scene_before_a_temple_facade_Late_Uruk_ca._3500%E2%80%933100_BCE.jpg

[35] Osama Shukir Muhammed Amin FRCP(Glasg), CC BY-SA 4.0 <https://creativecommons.org/licenses/by-sa/4.0>, via Wikimedia Commons https://commons.wikimedia.org/wiki/File:Goddess_Nisaba_with_the_name_of_Entemena_in_cuneiform._From_Iraq,_2430_BCE._Pergamon_Museum.jpg

[36] Osama Shukir Muhammed Amin FRCP(Glasg), CC BY-SA 4.0 <https://creativecommons.org/licenses/by-sa/4.0>, via Wikimedia Commons https://commons.wikimedia.org/wiki/File:A_replica_of_the_seated_statue_of_the_Sumerian_scribe_Dudu,_dedicated_to_god_Ningirsu._The_Sulaymaniyah_Museum.jpg

[37] British Museum, CC BY-SA 3.0 <https://creativecommons.org/licenses/by-sa/3.0>, via Wikimedia Commons https://commons.wikimedia.org/wiki/File:Library_of_Ashurbanipal_synonym_list_tablet.jpg

[38] British Museum, CC BY-SA 3.0 <https://creativecommons.org/licenses/by-sa/3.0>, via Wikimedia Commons https://commons.wikimedia.org/wiki/File:Royal_Game_of_Ur_rules.jpg

[39] Mefman00, CC0, via Wikimedia Commons https://commons.wikimedia.org/wiki/File:Enheduanna,_daughter_of_Sargon_of_Akkad.jpg

[40] Internet Archive Book Images, No restrictions, via Wikimedia Commons https://commons.wikimedia.org/wiki/File:Myths_and_legends_of_Babylonia_and_Assyria_(1916)_(14595422800).jpg

[41] Hamody al-Iraqi, CC BY-SA 4.0 <https://creativecommons.org/licenses/by-sa/4.0>, via Wikimedia Commons https://commons.wikimedia.org/wiki/File:Ishtar_gate_2.jpg

[42] Osama Shukir Muhammed Amin FRCP(Glasg), CC BY-SA 4.0
<https://creativecommons.org/licenses/by-sa/4.0>, via Wikimedia Commons
https://commons.wikimedia.org/wiki/File:Detail._A_high-ranking_neo-
Assyrian_official_wearing_a_diadem_(crown_prince%3F)._From_the_North-
West_of_Ashurnasipal_II_at_Nimrud,_Iraq._883-
859_BCE._Museum_of_the_Ancient_Orient,_Istanbul,_Turkey.jpg

[43] M.atkinson ross, CC BY-SA 4.0 <https://creativecommons.org/licenses/by-sa/4.0>, via
Wikimedia Commons
https://commons.wikimedia.org/wiki/File:The_Sumerian_King_List,_Ashmolean_Museum,_Oxf
ord.jpg

[44] पाटलिपुत्र, CC BY-SA 4.0 <https://creativecommons.org/licenses/by-sa/4.0>, via Wikimedia
Commons
https://commons.wikimedia.org/wiki/File:Mebaragsi,_King_of_Kish_(transcription_of_fragment,
_original_in_Iraq_National_Museum).jpg

[45] https://commons.wikimedia.org/wiki/File:Sumer.JPG

[46] Near_East_topographic_map-blank.svg: Sémhurderivative work: Zunkir, CC BY-SA 3.0
<https://creativecommons.org/licenses/by-sa/3.0>, via Wikimedia Commons
https://commons.wikimedia.org/wiki/File:Basse_Mesopotamie_DA.PNG

[47] File: Near East topographic map-blank.svg: SémhurFile:Elam-map-PL.svg: W Kotwica
Derivative work: Morningstar1814, CC BY-SA 3.0 <https://creativecommons.org/licenses/by-
sa/3.0>, via Wikimedia Commons https://commons.wikimedia.org/wiki/File:Elam_Map-en.svg

[48] https://commons.wikimedia.org/wiki/File:Kubaba_relief.JPG

[49] Once In Awhile, CC BY-SA 4.0 <https://creativecommons.org/licenses/by-sa/4.0>, via
Wikimedia Commons
https://commons.wikimedia.org/wiki/File:Ur_Namma_stele_Nanna_Penn_Museum.jpg

[50] A.Davey from Portland, Oregon, EE UU, CC BY 2.0
<https://creativecommons.org/licenses/by/2.0>, via Wikimedia Commons
https://commons.wikimedia.org/wiki/File:Ahura_Mazda_(right)_Invests_Ardashir_I_With_the_
Ring_of_Kingship_(4895917806).jpg

[51] https://commons.wikimedia.org/wiki/File:Hit,_Euphrates_Art.IWMART2353.jpg

[52] https://commons.wikimedia.org/wiki/File:C%2BB-Music-Fig24-AssyrianQuartet.PNG

[53] https://commons.wikimedia.org/wiki/File:Mesopotamian_-_Duck_-_Walters_421455.jpg

[54] Allan Gluck, CC BY 4.0 <https://creativecommons.org/licenses/by/4.0>, via Wikimedia
Commons https://commons.wikimedia.org/wiki/File:Assyrian_Relief_depicting_
Celebration_after_a_Royal_Bull_Hunt_Kalhu_(Nimrud)_Northwest_Palace_Ashurnasirpal_II_
875-860_BCE_British_Museum_AG.jpg

[55] https://commons.wikimedia.org/wiki/File:Mesopotamian_-
_Cylinder_Seal_with_a_Deity_Accepting_an_Offering_-_Walters_42713.jpg

[56] Artist Unknown, CC0, via Wikimedia Commons
https://commons.wikimedia.org/wiki/File:Assyrian_Furniture_panel_made_of_Ivory_and_Wood
.jpg

[57] Internet Archive Book Images, No restrictions, via Wikimedia Commons
https://commons.wikimedia.org/wiki/File:The_story_of_the_greatest_nations;_a_comprehensive_history,_extending_from_the_earliest_times_to_the_present,_founded_on_the_most_modern_authorities,_and_including_chronological_summaries_and_(14596654787).jpg

[58] Miguel Angel Omaña Rojas, CC BY 4.0 <https://creativecommons.org/licenses/by/4.0>, via Wikimedia Commons https://commons.wikimedia.org/wiki/File:Sumerian_Queen_Kubaba.jpg

[59] Sailko, CC BY 3.0 <https://creativecommons.org/licenses/by/3.0>, via Wikimedia Commons https://commons.wikimedia.org/wiki/File:Ishtar_on_an_Akkadian_seal.jpg

[60] Osama Shukir Muhammed Amin FRCP(Glasg), CC BY-SA 4.0 <https://creativecommons.org/licenses/by-sa/4.0>, via Wikimedia Commons https://commons.wikimedia.org/wiki/File:Detail._Part_of_the_so-called_Banquet_Plaques._Beer_was_a_common_daily_dietary_staple_in_ancient_Mesopotamia._From_Ur,_Iraq._Early_Dynastic_Period,_2900-2350_BCE._Sulaymaniyah_Museum,_Iraqi_Kurdistan.jpg

[61] Osama Shukir Muhammed Amin FRCP(Glasg), CC BY-SA 4.0 <https://creativecommons.org/licenses/by-sa/4.0>, via Wikimedia Commons https://commons.wikimedia.org/wiki/File:Ruins_of_the_ziggurat_and_temple_of_god_Nabu_at_the_ancient_city_of_Borsippa,_Babel_Governorate,_Iraq._6th_century_BC.jpg

[62] Merikanto, CC BY 4.0 <https://creativecommons.org/licenses/by/4.0>, via Wikimedia Commons https://commons.wikimedia.org/wiki/File:Choga_mami_on_near_east_precipitation_map_1.png

[63] Osama Shukir Muhammed Amin FRCP(Glasg), CC BY-SA 4.0 <https://creativecommons.org/licenses/by-sa/4.0>, via Wikimedia Commons https://commons.wikimedia.org/wiki/File:Terracotta_plaque_depicting_Mushussu_(Mu%C5%A1%E1%B8%ABu%C5%A1%C5%A1u;_sirrush)._This_model_plaque_was_mass-produced_at_that_time_to_protect_Babylonian_households_from_enemies._From_southern_Iraq._800-500_BCE.jpg

[64] Daderot, CC0, via Wikimedia Commons https://commons.wikimedia.org/wiki/File:Clay_peg_for_patterned_wall_decoration,_terracotta_-_Oriental_Institute_Museum,_University_of_Chicago_-_DSC07029.JPG

[65] Mary Harrsch, CC BY 2.0 <https://creativecommons.org/licenses/by/2.0>, via Wikimedia Commons https://commons.wikimedia.org/wiki/File:Two_female_figurines_with_bitumen_headdresses_ceramic_Ur_Iraq_Ubaid_4_period_4500-4000_BCE.jpg

[66] Osama Shukir Muhammed Amin FRCP(Glasg), CC BY-SA 4.0 <https://creativecommons.org/licenses/by-sa/4.0>, via Wikimedia Commons https://commons.wikimedia.org/wiki/File:Warka_Vase,_Top_Register.jpg

[67] David Stanley from Nanaimo, Canada, CC BY 2.0 <https://creativecommons.org/licenses/by/2.0>, via Wikimedia Commons https://commons.wikimedia.org/wiki/File:Hanging_Gardens_of_Babylon_(30309171040).jpg

[68] Osama Shukir Muhammed Amin, CC BY-SA 3.0 <https://creativecommons.org/licenses/by-sa/3.0>, via Wikimedia Commons https://commons.wikimedia.org/wiki/File:Foundation_Pegs,_from_Ningirsu_Temple,_Girsu.jpg

[69] ninara, CC BY-SA 2.0 <https://creativecommons.org/licenses/by-sa/2.0>, via Wikimedia Commons https://commons.wikimedia.org/wiki/File:Choqa_Zanbil_2.jpg

[70] Bertramz, CC BY 3.0 <https://creativecommons.org/licenses/by/3.0>, via Wikimedia Commons https://commons.wikimedia.org/wiki/File:TellBrakTW-W.jpg

[71] Osama Shukir Muhammed Amin FRCP(Glasg), CC BY-SA 4.0 <https://creativecommons.org/licenses/by-sa/4.0>, via Wikimedia Commons https://commons.wikimedia.org/wiki/File:Soldiers_of_Taharqa_defending_their_city_from_the_Assyrian_assault.jpg

[72] Osama Shukir Muhammed Amin FRCP(Glasg), CC BY-SA 4.0 <https://creativecommons.org/licenses/by-sa/4.0>, via Wikimedia C https://commons.wikimedia.org/wiki/File:Stele_of_Adad-nirari_III.jpg

[73] Zunkir, CC BY-SA 4.0 <https://creativecommons.org/licenses/by-sa/4.0>, via Wikimedia Commons https://commons.wikimedia.org/wiki/File:Cylinder_seal_Ur_III_BM_89131.jpg

[74] https://commons.wikimedia.org/wiki/File:Mod%C3%A8le_de_chariot_de_guerre_-_Kish_-_P%C3%A9riode_Pal%C3%A9o_babylonienne.jpg

[75] Anonymous, CC BY-SA 4.0 <https://creativecommons.org/licenses/by-sa/4.0>, via Wikimedia Commons https://commons.wikimedia.org/wiki/File:The_Akkadian_Empire.png

[76] Gary Todd, CC0, via Wikimedia Commons https://commons.wikimedia.org/wiki/File:Meskalamdug_helmet_back_view.jpg

[77] The original uploader was Artaxiad at English Wikipedia., CC BY-SA 3.0 <http://creativecommons.org/licenses/by-sa/3.0/>, via Wikimedia Commons https://commons.wikimedia.org/wiki/File:13-Urartu-9-6mta.gif

[78] https://commons.wikimedia.org/wiki/File:Assyrian_archers.jpg

[79] British Museum, CC BY 2.5 <https://creativecommons.org/licenses/by/2.5>, via Wikimedia Commons https://commons.wikimedia.org/wiki/File:Tiglath-pileser_III_BM_WA118900.jpg

[80] Mary Harrsch from Springfield, Oregon, USA, CC BY 2.0 <https://creativecommons.org/licenses/by/2.0>, via Wikimedia Commons https://commons.wikimedia.org/wiki/File:Statue_of_Ashurbanipal_outside_the_Asian_Art_Museum_1_(261590353).jpg

[81] https://commons.wikimedia.org/wiki/File:Mesopotamian_-_Barrel-Shaped_Cylinder_Seal_-_Walters_42655.jpg

[82] © Marie-Lan Nguyen / Wikimedia Commons https://commons.wikimedia.org/wiki/File:Silver_debt_tablet_and_envelope_IAM.jpg

[83] Gary Todd from Xinzheng, China, CC0, via Wikimedia Commons https://commons.wikimedia.org/wiki/File:Ancient_Assyria_Jewelry_(28672549256).jpg

[84] Eric Polk, CC BY-SA 4.0 <https://creativecommons.org/licenses/by-sa/4.0>, via Wikimedia Commons https://commons.wikimedia.org/wiki/File:Persian_daric_with_king_holding_bow.jpg

[85] Mary Harrsch, CC BY 2.0 <https://creativecommons.org/licenses/by/2.0>, via Wikimedia Commonshttps://commons.wikimedia.org/wiki/File:Ancient_Mesopotamian_Counting_Tokens_from_Tepe_Gawra_in_modern_day_Iraq_5000-4500_BCE.jpg

[86] Osama Shukir Muhammed Amin FRCP(Glasg), CC BY-SA 4.0
<https://creativecommons.org/licenses/by-sa/4.0>, via Wikimedia Commons
https://commons.wikimedia.org/wiki/File:One_of_the_Amarna_letters._Correspondence_betwe
en_a_king_of_Alashiya_and_Amenhotep_III_of_Egypt._Circa_1380_BCE._From_Tell_el-
Amarna,_Egypt._Vorderasiatisches_Museum,_Berlin.jpg

[87] Middle_East_topographic_map-blank.svg: Sémhur (talk)derivative work: Zunkir, CC BY-SA
3.0 <https://creativecommons.org/licenses/by-sa/3.0>, via Wikimedia Commons
https://commons.wikimedia.org/wiki/File:Moyen_Orient_3mil_aC.svg

[88] Osama Shukir Muhammed Amin FRCP(Glasg), CC BY-SA 4.0
<https://creativecommons.org/licenses/by-sa/4.0>, via Wikimedia Commons
https://commons.wikimedia.org/wiki/File:Lizard-
headed_nude_woman_nursing_a_child,_from_Ur,_Iraq,_c._4000_BCE._Iraq_Museum_(retouc
hed).jpg

[89] Joshua Doubek, CC BY-SA 3.0 <https://creativecommons.org/licenses/by-sa/3.0>, via
Wikimedia Commons https://commons.wikimedia.org/wiki/File:Zagros_Folded_Zone.jpg

[90] Daderot, CC0, via Wikimedia Commons
https://commons.wikimedia.org/wiki/File:Metal_coils_of_silver_used_for_currency,_Mesopotam
ia_-_Oriental_Institute_Museum,_University_of_Chicago_-_DSC07273.JPG

[91] Sam Valadi, CC BY 2.0 <https://creativecommons.org/licenses/by/2.0>, via Wikimedia
Commons https://commons.wikimedia.org/wiki/File:Guggenheim_Museum-
_New_York_City_(17207156426).jpg

[92] https://commons.wikimedia.org/wiki/File:Sumerian_pre-cuneiform_number_system.gif

[93] A.Davey from Portland, Oregon, EE UU, CC BY 2.0
<https://creativecommons.org/licenses/by/2.0>, via Wikimedia Commons
https://commons.wikimedia.org/wiki/File:The_Gilgamesh_Pot_(4769119820).jpg

[94] https://commons.wikimedia.org/wiki/File:Ethel_Birch_-_Cherwell,_Mesopotamia_-
_Sarjeant_Gallery.jpg

[95] Avveroes, CC BY-SA 3.0 <https://creativecommons.org/licenses/by-sa/3.0>, via Wikimedia
Commons https://commons.wikimedia.org/wiki/File:Dia-Al-Azzawi-Portrait-Picture.jpg

[96] Internet Archive Book Images, No restrictions, via Wikimedia Commons
https://commons.wikimedia.org/wiki/File:The_popular_and_critical_Bible_encyclop%C3%A6dia
_and_Scriptural_dictionary,_fully_defining_and_explaining_all_religious_terms,_including_biogr
aphical,_geographical,_historical,_archaeological_and_doctrinal_(14756078436).jpg

[97] Alemazzi, CC BY-SA 4.0 <https://creativecommons.org/licenses/by-sa/4.0>, via Wikimedia
Commons
https://commons.wikimedia.org/wiki/File:Mesopotamian_hybrid_beings_(Mischwesen)_by_Fran
s_A.M._Wiggermann.png

[98] LittleAstronomer, CC BY-SA 4.0 <https://creativecommons.org/licenses/by-sa/4.0>, via
Wikimedia Commons https://commons.wikimedia.org/wiki/File:Leo%2Bhya_mul-apin.jpg

[99] https://commons.wikimedia.org/wiki/File:Well%26Karez.JPG

[100] w_lemay, CC BY-SA 2.0 <https://creativecommons.org/licenses/by-sa/2.0>, via Wikimedia Commons https://commons.wikimedia.org/wiki/File:Rookery_Building,_LaSalle_Street_and_Adams_Street,_Chicago,_IL_-_52901591410.jpg

Printed in Great Britain
by Amazon

59333306R00136